OTHER BOOKS BY TRAILER LIFE

An RVer's Annual: The Best of Trailer Life and Motorhome
Edited by Rena Copperman

This collector's edition of the best travel, technical, personality, and feature articles from past issues of the magazines, acknowledged as the leading publications in the RV field, is topped off with a special "Constitution" feature, recalling the recent nationwide anniversary celebration in prose and pictures. Beautiful four-color photos throughout . . . a great gift idea.
8½×11, 208 pages
$15.95 ISBN: 0-934798-21-4

Full-time RVing: A Complete Guide to Life on the Open Road
Bill and Jan Moeller

The answers to all the questions anyone who dreams of traveling full time in an RV may have can be found in this remarkable new source book. *Full-time RVing* takes the mystery out of fulltiming and makes it possible to fully enjoy this once-in-a-lifetime experience.
7¼×9¼, 352 pages
$14.95 ISBN: 0-934798-14-1

RX for RV Performance & Mileage
John Geraghty and Bill Estes

In 32 chapters, this book covers everything an owner must know about how an engine (particularly a V-8) works, vehicle maintenance, propane and diesel as alternative fuels, eliminating engine "ping," improving exhaust systems and fuel economy, and much more.
7¾×9¼, 359 pages
$14.95 ISBN: 0-934798-08-0

The Good Sam RV Cookbook
Edited by Beverly Edwards and the editors of *Trailer Life*

Over 250 easy and delicious recipes, including 78 prize-winners from Good Sam Samboree cook-offs around the country. Also contains tips, ideas, and suggestions to help you get the most from your RV galley.
7¼×9¼, 252 pages
$14.95 ISBN: 0-934798-17-6

These books are available at fine bookstores everywhere. Or, you may order directly from Trailer Life. For each book ordered, simply send us the name of the book, the price, plus $2 per book for shipping and handling (California residents please add 6½% sales tax). Mail to:

Trailer Life Books, P.O. Box 4500, Agoura, CA 91301

You may call our Customer Service representatives if you wish to charge your order or if you want more information. Please phone, toll-free, Monday through Friday, 7:00 A.M. to 6:00 P.M.; Saturday, 7:30 A.M. to 12:30 P.M. Pacific Time, **1-800-234-3450.**

RVing America's Backroads:
Idaho & Montana

Robert Longsdorf, Jr.

. . . Light-hearted I take to the open road,
Healthy, free, the world before me,
The long brown path before me leading
wherever I choose."

Walt Whitman, *Song of the Open Road*

Trailer Life Books
Agoura, California

Trailer Life Book Division

President: Richard Rouse
Vice President/General Manager: Ted Binder
Vice President/Publisher, Book Division: Michael Schneider
General Manager, Book Division: Rena Copperman
Assistant Manager, Book Division: Cindy Lang

Cover design: Bob Schroeder
Cover photograph: Robert Longsdorf, Jr.
Interior design: David Fuller/Robert S. Tinnon
Production manager: Rena Copperman
Editorial assistant: Judi Lazarus
Indexer: Barbara Wurf
Maps: EarthSurface Graphics

This book was set in ITC Garamond Book by Publisher's
Typography and printed on 60-pound Consoweb Brilliant by
R.R. Donnelley and Sons in Willard, Ohio.

Library of Congress Cataloging-in-Publication Data

Longsdorf, Robert, 1941–
    RVing America's backroads: Idaho & Montana.

    Includes index.
    1. Automobiles—Idaho—Touring.   2. Recreational
vehicles—Idaho.   3. Idaho—Description and travel—
1981–   —Guide-books.   4. Automobiles—Montana—
Touring.   5. Recreational vehicles—Montana.
6. Montana—Description and travel—1981–   —Guide-
books.   I. Title.
GV1024.L575   1989   917.86   86–50523
ISBN 0–934798–13–3

Contents

OTHER BOOKS BY TRAILER LIFE

Full-time RVing: A Complete Guide to Life on the Open Road
Bill and Jan Moeller

The answers to all the questions anyone who dreams of traveling full time in an RV may have can be found in this remarkable new source book. *Full-time RVing* takes the mystery out of fulltiming and makes it possible to fully enjoy this once-in-a-lifetime experience.
7¼×9¼, 352 pages
$14.95 ISBN: 0-934798-14-1

RX for RV Performance & Mileage
John Geraghty and Bill Estes

In 32 chapters, this book covers everything an owner must know about how an engine (particularly a V-8) works, vehicle maintenance, propane and diesel as alternative fuels, eliminating engine "ping," improving exhaust systems and fuel economy, and much more.
7¾×9¼, 359 pages
$14.95 ISBN: 0-934798-08-0

The RV Galley Cookbook
Edited by Beverly Edwards and the editors of *Trailer Life*

Over 250 easy and delicious recipes, including 78 prize-winners from Good Sam Samboree cook-offs around the country. Also contains tips, ideas, and suggestions to help you get the most from your RV galley.
7¼×9¼, 252 pages
$14.95 ISBN: 0-934798-17-6

These books are available at fine bookstores everywhere. Or, you may order directly from Trailer Life. For each book ordered, simply send us the name of the book, the price, plus $2 per book for shipping and handling (California residents please add 6½% sales tax). Mail to:

Trailer Life Books, P.O. Box 4500, Agoura, CA 91301

You may call our Customer Service representatives if you wish to charge your order or if you want more information. Please phone, toll-free, Monday through Friday, 7:00 A.M. to 6:00 P.M.; Saturday, 7:30 A.M. to 12:30 P.M. Pacific Time, **1-800-234-3450.**

Preface

I have always maintained that RVers are the last pioneers. Within each of us is the same spirit of adventure and the burning curiosity that motivated the early settlers to strike out for the Western Territories, to see what lies over the next hill, to explore the unknown.

For RVers in whom that spirit is especially strong, Idaho and Montana is your country. Here you'll find wide-open spaces, a rich western heritage, and constant reminders of the struggle between the white man and the Indian for domination of the territory. In each town, you'll find numerous tales recounting the lawless days of the frontier, when justice often came swiftly.

There are clear, cool mountain streams, rushing rivers with some of the nation's best white-water rapids, as well as shaded, pine-scented campgrounds tucked in deep recesses of the vast national forests, parks, and state and federal recreation areas that abound here. RVers will also find the majestic Rocky Mountains and the magnificent Sawtooth, Lost River and Clearwater ranges. For the early pioneers these peaks represented formidable barriers on the road west. For travelers in today's modern RVs they offer sweeping vistas as well as a host of backroad valleys and picturesque byways awaiting exploration.

To make your visit to this region more enjoyable I have selected what I consider to be some of the best backroad routes to be found. While these routes were originally developed from my random travels and meanderings through these states, ultimately I relied heavily on information gathered from local chambers of commerce, state tourism officials and, finally, and perhaps most importantly, from the valued tips and suggestions of the native residents whose hospitality and eagerness to share the riches of their region helped me to discover many of the backroad treasures listed here.

I would like to give special thanks to the Department of Commerce of the State of Montana and the Idaho State Historical Society for their generous help in providing additional photographs to illustrate the book.

Bear in mind that while every attempt has been made to assure that information on routes, road conditions, entrance fees and other factual matter was accurate at press time, inevitably things change. Therefore, as you retrace my route and follow in my footsteps I urge you to draw upon these same sources to supplement this guide.

To those final words of advice I can only add that I hope that you find this book of value in your travels and that its pages will provide you with the same sensations of discovery and joy that I found in the research and writing.

IDAHO

"... A lot of state this Idaho, that I didn't know about," Ernest Hemingway wrote in 1939. Things haven't changed much since then; nearly fifty years later Idaho remains largely undiscovered.

Idaho seems made for backroad explorers. With a total state population of less than one million, and some 82,000 square miles of land mass—70 percent publicly-owned—Idaho is an uncrowded paradise waiting to be discovered by RVers. The tours outlined here capture the essence of that undiscovered Idaho, from the high desert country of the southwest to the high peaks of the Sawtooth and Seven Devils mountain ranges. These backroads will also take you to North America's deepest chasm, the 7,900-foot Hells Canyon, and back into history to the gold rush of the 1860s and the Nez Perce Indian Wars.

As you make your way along these routes, you'll discover one of Idaho's other natural resources, its people. They'll not only welcome you to their state and communities, they'll delight you with some unusual entertainment—old-time fiddle contests, winter carnivals, sheepherder festivals, rodeos, Indian pow-wows, and a host of other celebrations.

You're urged to get off the beaten path and explore Idaho's majestic scenery and backroad delights. The natives point with pride to the Gem State's treasures and say that it's only natural that Hemingway found the lure of its green velvet vistas irresistible, that Chief Joseph sought it as a refuge for his people, that Lewis and Clark and the French explorers lingered so long in its lush river valleys. And, they promise, you too will feel the exultation of Idaho's high mountains, the strength of its moving waters, and the spirit of peace to be found in a backcountry campground.

The Sawtooth Loop

The day's bone dry.
I've come through Sun Valley
To sit beside your rock and your greening bust
Above the Big Lost River
Where sage and bitterbrush and broom
Have held their own, where the cicadas
Chirr through the cottonwoods in
the dead of summer.

—David Wagoner, *At the Hemingway Memorial*

It was Hemingway country that originally drew me to Idaho's Saw-tooths. I wanted to see Ketchum and Sun Valley, the rugged mountains, clear blue skies, and sparkling trout streams that originally brought the famous writer and outdoorsman here in 1958. What I didn't realize was that this small area in the southeastern Sawtooth foothills represents only a fraction of what has to be counted as one of Idaho's most scenic and historically interesting regions.

My trip along the Sawtooth Loop began in Boise in the early fall, when I stopped off to see Bobbie Patterson, executive director of Boise Convention and Visitors' Bureau. When I spread out my map marked with potential destinations, Bobbie said, "If you're going to Ketchum and Sun Valley, you've got to go the back way, up behind the Saw-tooths, through Idaho City, Lowman, and Stanley. It's some of the best scenery in the whole state, and especially beautiful this time of year."

So the next morning, following the route Bobbie sketched out on my map, I headed out of Boise on a small side road that winds east of the city, just north of I-84. A couple of miles outside of town, I stopped at the U.S. Forest Service office to gather information on the Sawtooth and Boise National Forests, which, combined, sprawl across nearly 4.5 million acres of the Sawtooth region. As it turned out, the office had a wealth of background material, including two excellent maps titled: *Travel Plan: Sawtooth National Forest* and *Travel Plan: Boise National Forest*. Both maps offered detailed information on trails and backroads in the area.

Along with the maps came some advice on road conditions. Seeing my 35-foot motorhome sitting out front, the office manager was a bit worried about a pending storm and how well the rig would navigate some of the unpaved backroads. After assuring her I would be careful, I headed out, picking up SR 21, and turning north toward the distant mountains.

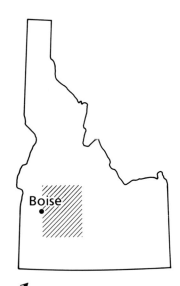

Tour **1** *272 miles*

BOISE • LUCKY PEAK RESERVOIR • WARM SPRINGS • IDAHO CITY • NEW CENTERVILLE • CENTERVILLE • PLACERVILLE • PIONERVILLE • LOWMAN • KIRKHAM HOT SPRINGS • GRANDJEAN • CAPE HORN • STANLEY • SUN VALLEY • KETCHUM • HAILEY • BELLEVUE

Up Behind the Sawtooths

As I started the climb up past Lucky Peak Reservoir and Discovery State Park, I began to wonder where all the magnificent scenery was that I was supposed to find along this route. The surrounding countryside for as far as I could see was high desert terrain. Even the narrow channels of the middle and south forks of the Boise River were fairly devoid of greenery. In a few miles, though, as the road began to take a steeper climb and narrowed to just two lanes, I rounded a bend and looked ahead to thickening stands of Ponderosa pines and the blazing fall colors of aspens and cottonwoods. In no time at all I was deep in thick forest and climbing steadily into the mountain chill.

A Fitting Tribute.
The Hemingway Memorial stands as a fitting tribute to the famed author-sportsman in the country he loved above all.

Idaho's First Penitentiary.
Sheriff John Leary poses in front of the Idaho Penitentiary in 1912 with what appear to be two "residents," identified as Joe Dandy and Jeff Sayer. (*Idaho State Historical Society*)

Idaho City, 1894.
This view of Main and Commercial was taken in Idaho City on April 15, 1894. In the foreground a family proudly pose in their front yard. (*Idaho City Historical Foundation*)

The Forest Service personnel have a saying here that summer doesn't come to the Sawtooths until July, and winter starts in August. In late September, with a decided nip in the air and with the hardwoods rapidly losing their colorful foliage, it seemed like winter was well under way. By the time I reached the outskirts of Idaho City, the sky was a leaden overcast. With weather closing in, even though it was only early afternoon, I decided to stop at the Warm Springs resort, a private campground that takes its name from the natural hot springs that have been piped into a large pool kept at a steaming 97 degrees year round. Since the resort offered full hookups and owner Dick Weibye proved to be a good source of information on nearby points of interest, I decided to make the campground my base for a couple of days' exploration of an area that played such a pivotal role in Idaho's gold rush era.

Idaho City—Reduced from Its Glory Days

The next morning, with the fall storm clouds still hanging heavy over the mountains, I rolled two miles north to Idaho City. Looking at the small community that covers only four square blocks, with a current population of only 300, it is hard to imagine that this town was once the largest city in the Northwest. At the height of Idaho's gold rush in 1865, the town boasted a population of more than 35,000 and a busy main street that stretched for blocks.

Now, with Idaho City considerably reduced from its glory days, it's the perfect size for a walking tour along its gravel streets and wooden sidewalks. For RVers, that tour must start at the parking lot just off Wall Street, next to the Old Idaho Territorial Penitentiary, the only lot in town large enough to accommodate RVs. After I parked the motorhome, my first stop was the old prison, where the log walls of the cramped quarters are covered with carvings left by the prisoners more than 100 years ago. From the prison it's just a few steps across the road to a small park where a collection of mining equipment and artifacts are displayed in outdoor exhibits.

On Montgomery Street I stopped in the Idaho City Hotel and picked up a walking tour map. I also met Don Campbell, proprietor of the hotel, who accompanied me on part of my walk through town. As Don pointed out some of the more interesting old structures, he also told me about the devastating fires that swept through Idaho City between 1865 and 1871. Those fires, which caused more than a million dollars in damage, were perhaps as much responsible for the town's decline as the diminishing returns of the nearby gold fields.

Despite the ravages of the fires, several original structures still remain. Among these are the Masonic Temple on Wall Street, the oldest Masonic Hall west of the Mississippi still in use; the former James Pinney bookstore and post office (Central News Depot), built in 1867, which now houses the Boise Basin Museum; the white, wooden St. Joseph Catholic Church, the first Catholic church for the white population in Idaho, which sits high atop a steep hill overlooking Main Street; and the one-story brick Boise Basin Mercantile, on Main Street, Idaho's oldest existing store. There's also the *Idaho World* newspaper office, now housed in an old building about a block from the original site.

Backroads of Idaho City

With so much of Idaho's—and the Northwest's—history wrapped up in this one section of the Sawtooths, I was anxious to explore some of the backroad areas behind Idaho City, where much of the mining actually

Masonic Temple.
This structure, located on Wall Street, is the oldest Masonic Hall west of the Mississippi still in use. (*Idaho State Historical Society*)

Boise Basin Mercantile.
Two unidentified gentlemen (probably the proprietor and his assistant) are seen in Idaho's oldest existing store in this photo. Situated on Main Street, the store sold clothes, food, and tools to the populace of Idaho City. (*Idaho State Historical Society*)

St. Joseph Church.
The beautiful white wooden building was the first Catholic church for the white population in Idaho.

Idaho World.
A closer look at the offices of this
historic newspaper with former editor
Jody Bickle.

took place. Although I had been warned that some of the dirt roads
west of Idaho City were not appropriate for large motorhomes, I decided to drive as far as I could out the Centerville Road to Placerville,
Centerville, and New Centerville. The going was slow, but proved to
be worth the effort.

New Centerville and Its Environs

About seven miles due west of Idaho City, I came across New Centerville, once an important timber town and the southern terminus for
the old Intermountain Railway. A few miles northwest I found Placer-

Taking the Backroad.
The road outside of Idaho City is difficult driving for large motorhomes, but worth the effort.

Placerville Dwelling.
The resident of this cabin, identified as Mr. William Cowden, Sr., is shown seated in front of his home in 1917. (*Idaho State Historical Society*)

ville, the site of the first camp for miners who came to seek their fortune in the Boise basin. Although Placerville is now practically deserted, the Henrietta Penrod Museum, housed in what was once a fancy bar called the Magnolia Saloon, is definitely worth a stop.

As in many of the Western states, a lot of the history of the Idaho City gold rush era can be read on the tombstones in the old cemeteries found here. Besides the main cemetery, which lies at the western edge of Idaho City, the community cemetery one mile south of Placer-

Magnolia Saloon.
The historic Magnolia Saloon in Placerville houses the Henrietta Penrod Museum, worth a stop to the traveler. (*Idaho State Historical Society*)

ville proved to be a rich source of local lore. A small concrete marker with the inscription "Fiddlers Murdered in Ophir Creek" is testimony to one of the region's more colorful stories.

History records that in 1863 two fiddlers who had played for a dance in Placerville were traveling south to a similar engagement in Centerville. Midway they apparently stumbled on the murder of a miner, killed for his gold. To assure that no witnesses remained, the murderer also dispatched the fiddlers. Shortly after the three bodies were discovered, a local horse thief and general ne'er-do-well, John Williams, was arrested and charged with the crime. In a strange twist of justice, however, Williams escaped punishment because of a legal technicality. His lawyers found that at the time of the crime, Idaho had no criminal law because Congress had failed to enact a new territorial code when the Idaho Territory was established. The Idaho chief justice had no choice but to set Williams free. Upon his release Williams promptly disappeared, never to be heard from again.

Moving On—Lowman

By the time I finished my explorations of Idaho City's backcountry, the storm clouds looked as if they had moved in to stay and I decided it was time to move on. Under darkening skies I rolled back through town and turned north on SR 21, just in time to catch the first flakes of an early fall snow on my windshield. As I continued to climb toward Mores Creek Summit (6,118 feet) the snowfall increased, covering the red and yellow fall leaves and road with a light dusting of white.

But just as fast as it had begun, the storm swept on. By the time I started down the other side of the summit, only an occasional flake was hitting the windshield, and off in the distance patches of blue could be seen returning to the sky. Although the odometer indicated I had only covered about 35 miles since leaving Idaho City, the storm and a few stops to take in the scenery of the river valley and distant mountains had made the going very slow.

A few miles after clearing the summit, I came upon the sign marking the outskirts of Lowman, a town so remote that it didn't get phone service until 1982. Just beyond the sign, the South Fork Lodge, a pleasant little campground in a scenic valley setting on the Payette River, appeared on the left. It seemed an ideal spot to lay over and let the storm clouds pass.

After hooking up, I wandered up the hill to the South Fork's restaurant where I met Ellen Shaw, who, with her husband, owns and operates the campground, motel, and a fine restaurant. Over a dinner of fresh rainbow trout, Ellen filled me in on some of the local points of interest. She also told me that despite the excellent fishing in the area and the magnificent scenery, this area, like much of Idaho, was relatively undiscovered and free of crowds during the peak tourist season.

1. Martin Cathcart, Boots and Shoes   4. J. W. Davidson, Hotel.   7. Halley & Donivan, Saloon.   10. Magnolia Saloon,
2. Michael Halley.   5. Rogan & Spencer, Grocery.   8. Mrs. Stickler, Phœnix Hotel.   J. McKay, Proprietor.
3. Wagner & McDavitt s Building.   6. John Nelson, Saloon.   9. Wagner & McDavitt, Empire Market   11. Shelley & Co., Livery.

PUBLIC SQUARE and Surrounding PLACES OF BUSINESS, PLACERVILLE, Idaho.

Old Placerville.
Although almost all that remains today is the Magnolia Saloon (*far right*), in 1894
Placerville boasted three salons and two hotels among its buildings. (*Source:* W. Elliott,
History of Idaho Territory)

As I had passed a number of deserted campgrounds along the way, it
seemed obvious that the area was indeed unknown to many RVers.
"And that's really a shame," Ellen said. "We've got so much to offer
here, especially this time of year. Right now it's unseasonably cold, but
usually this is our Indian summer, when the trees are turning and
when the fishing is just starting to get good."

The next morning, after working my way through a breakfast that
included two huge, freshly baked hot cinnamon buns—a morning specialty at the lodge restaurant—I decided to take Ellen's advice and do
some exploring along the Garden Valley Road. This dirt route leads
west out of Lowman and winds back along the Payette River, through

some of the Boise National Forest's most magnificent scenery. Thanks to the rain and snow of the previous day, the road wasn't in the best of shape, although a road crew was already at work smoothing out many of the rough spots. After about five miles of very slow traveling, I decided the route in its current condition was just not suitable for a large rig and turned around. When I returned to Lowman I learned that the road was being worked, not merely for maintenance, but to prepare it for a more permanent surface in the spring. The road is much improved now and would definitely be worth a second try.

Kirkham Hot Springs—A Hot Tub Delight

A second night at the South Fork campground and I headed north once again. Rounding a bend four miles north of Lowman, I was immediately struck by what appeared to be a isolated heavy fog hanging over Kirkham Hot Springs campground, a U.S. Forest Service facility situated on the banks of the Payette River. A spectacular sight in the early morning light, I couldn't resist the picture opportunities here.

Kirkham Hot Springs.
A U.S. Forest Service campground, located on the banks of the Payette River, Kirkham Hot Springs offers natural, hot therapeutic pools.

From the road the fog had appeared to be simply the result of the morning sun warming the moist ground. But, as I walked farther along the high banks of the river I suddenly realized the air here was much warmer than it had been when I alighted from the motorhome in the parking lot. Looking down through the mist, I could see small rivulets of water trickling along the ground and spilling over into the river. Reaching down, I found the water was extremely hot. I was walking across a field of hot water, and what I thought was fog was actually steam rising off of the overflow of a natural hot springs with temperatures of well over 100°. On closer inspection I could see that all along the river, rocks had been placed to capture this water in natural hot pools. Wandering further through the campground I also found a small shelter put up by the Forest Service that houses four tubs available without charge on a first-come-first-serve basis.

Grandjean Detour

The thought of a relaxing dip was tempting, but I decided to travel on to get an early morning view of the Sawtooth's western silhouette. About 20 miles north of the campground that opportunity presented itself with the turnoff to the tiny backcountry hamlet of Grandjean. Situated about five miles east of SR 21, at the end of a dirt road, Grandjean is an excellent stopover for RVers who really like to get away from it all. Besides its proximity to some excellent fishing on the Payette, Grandjean sits in the middle of the Boise National Forest, a remote location that makes it an ideal base for hikers and backpackers. For those who just want to kick back and relax, there is a campground at the Sawtooth Lodge, with a couple of hot springs nearby.

What the Grandjean detour also offers, though, is one of the most scenic drives to be found along this tour—and one of the first unobstructed views of the Sawtooths. Almost immediately after taking the turnoff to Grandjean, I came to a small spur road that dipped down into a wide valley. By driving just a short distance into the valley, I was able to get a sweeping view of the Sawtooth range off in the east. With the morning light beginning to rise above the mountains amid a growing bank of clouds, the scene was magnificent.

Briefly stopping in Grandjean, I returned to the highway and turned north once again, crossing Banner Summit (7,056 feet). About 15 miles north of the Grandjean road, a sign marking the turnoff to Dagger Falls appeared. Although the brochure from the state tourism office indicated this gravel route was an exceptionally scenic drive into Bear Valley and the headwaters of the Middle Fork of the Salmon River, I decided to pass up this detour in order to reach Stanley by nightfall. But I marked it as a must for my next trip, as the brochure indicated that the road is especially scenic in the spring wildflower season.

Shortly after passing the Dagger Falls turnoff, I came to another sign marking a side route to the small town of Cape Horn. At that point

Grandjean is named for Emil Charley Grandjean, a Danish immigrant whose father was Chamber Councilor of Forestry to the Danish king. He became Idaho's state supervisor of the Boise National Forest.

Grandjean Splendor.
One can observe the great Sawtooths
from the Stanley Lake road.

SR 21 takes a sharp turn to the south where it eventually links up with
SR 75 at the wild and woolly Old West town of Stanley. Here, as the
road begins to drop into the Stanley basin, the Sawtooths loom closer,
until just about five miles before coming into town the mountains' jagged profile becomes fully visible off to the right.

One of the best places to view the scenic splendor of the Sawtooths
here is from the shores of Stanley Lake. So I decided to make the lake,
an RVer's paradise, my stop for the night. In addition to three campgrounds at the lake there are boat concessions and, though I didn't get

Stanley Lake View.
One of the best spots for an unobstructed view of the Sawtooths is from the shores of
Stanley Lake.

a chance to try my luck, the lake is said to have excellent fishing for
Dolly Varden and rainbow trout.

The next morning I awoke to a magnificent sunrise reflecting off the
mountains and highlighting the mist rising out of the lake. The result
was a pastel panorama that was one of the most breathtaking sights of
the whole trip. Despite the magnificence of the scene, my schedule
called for me to push on, so reluctantly I pulled up stakes and headed
into Stanley.

During a quick stop in town for fuel, I learned that travelers proceeding south into the Sawtooth National Recreation Area could pick
up a cassette and recorder at the Forest Service's Stanley Ranger Station—and so I did. The recorded program, that one returns at the recreation headquarters office further south, provides a running
commentary on the surrounding area, noting geologic and geographic
points of interest of the Sawtooths. As the tape points out, the jagged
peaks of the Sawtooth range are 30 miles long and 15 miles wide.
Tucked into the small valleys between the mountains' rocky spires, of
which 78 rise more than 10,000 feet, are some 300 crystal-clear lakes.

Sheep Watch.
A Basque shepherd outside of Ketchum tends sheep with his trusty dog.

Stanley, on a Saturday night, vibrates with the music of a loud, western band that attracts cowboys, loggers, dudes, and anyone else within miles. Saloons, stores, and a hotel face the main (unpaved) street, the Ace of Diamonds.

From this range comes the snowmelt that forms the Salmon River, dubbed the "River of No Return" because for years its rapids made navigation upstream impossible. Because of those rapids, the Salmon today is one of the most popular whitewater rivers in the country. The intrepid outdoorsman or woman has plenty of opportunities to sample the Salmon's whitewater thrills by booking a raft trip of one to four days' duration through one of the local outfitters. The names, addresses, and phone numbers of outfitters are listed in the various brochures available at the ranger station or restaurants and shops around Stanley (see also page 21).

Rolling out of Stanley, I hadn't traveled very far before coming to the turnoff to Redfish Lake, probably the most popular recreation area in the Stanley basin. Although I didn't plan a stop here, curiosity about the area prompted me to take the time to pull in and see what it had to offer. Unlike Stanley Lake, Redfish is a huge body of water that stretches fingerlike back to the base of the Sawtooths. Like the other lakes in the area, however, Redfish is also reported to offer excellent trout fishing. RVing anglers who want to linger a few days to try their luck have plenty of opportunities to hook up in one of the several campgrounds. There are also some good restaurants and a visitor center that features interesting exhibits on local flora and fauna, as well as the geologic history of the area.

All along the route here there are small gravel side roads that beckon travelers to detour off the main highway and explore the backcountry. I chose one of those roads at random and had the good fortune to come across a Basque shepherd's camp only about a mile east of the highway. Although he couldn't speak any English, and I wasn't conversant in his native tongue, we spent a delightful half-hour talking in sign language. I left with a great respect for his willingness to follow such a rugged and lonely life-style.

Though I couldn't stay over, I was glad I took the time to stop so that I would have an idea of what was available for a return trip. After chatting with one of the residents in the area, I made a mental note to schedule that return for early spring or the fall months when the peak summer tourist season had passed. In view of the popularity of the Redfish Lake facilities in the summer, it seems advisable for RVers to call ahead to check on campground space. (Refer to the Stanley, Idaho, listings in *Trailer Life's RV Campground and Services Directory.*)

A few miles south of the Redfish turnoff, SR 75 begins its climb out of the valley over the Galena summit (8,701 feet), marking the divide between the Wood River and Salmon River drainages. Near the summit I pulled off into the view area to get one last good look at the Sawtooths before dropping down into the Wood River Valley.

Well into the valley I began to notice an increasing proliferation of high-priced vacation homes—a marked change from the remote and sparsely populated region I had just left, and the first clear signal that I was approaching the Ketchum/Sun Valley area.

Ketchum/Sun Valley Resort Area

Possessing the RVer's characteristic disdain for crowds and the hectic pace of civilization, I rolled into Ketchum prepared for the worst. I was pleasantly surprised to find a quiet and peaceful little town. It seemed a perfect time to visit. The summer crowds had long since gone and

Fisherman's Paradise.
The scenic woodriver, one of Hemingway's favorite trout streams, cascades through Ketchum/Sun Valley.

Ketchum was taking a breather before bracing for the onslaught of the Sun Valley ski season. After booking a campsite at the KOA south of town I still had plenty of time for a little exploration of Ketchum's attractions.

I was pleased to find that Ketchum still retains a certain rustic appeal, although it definitely also reflects the sophistication one would expect to find in a town so close to a world-class resort. After browsing through some of Ketchum's pleasant little shops, I couldn't resist sampling the fare at the Kneadery (260 Leadville Avenue), a rustic little restaurant which displays the work of some of the area's talented photographers. The food is good, moderately-priced American fare.

Hemingway Memorial.
A simple stone marker bears the words Hemingway had originally written as a eulogy for a friend but ironically became his own epitaph.

The next morning I headed east out of Ketchum on Sun Valley Road for the short drive into Sun Valley. Along the way, although I'm not a ski enthusiast, I took the time to detour down Dollar Road to the site of the original chair lift installed on Dollar Mountain in the days when Sun Valley was just gearing up as a world-class ski resort. Returning to the main route, a little farther on I passed more of Sun Valley's early history, the original Sun Valley Lodge. Beyond that, as Sun Valley Road winds into the open countryside east of town, I came to the turnoff to one of the main reasons for my trip, the Ernest Hemingway Memorial. After parking the motorhome, I walked the quiet path alongside Trail Creek to the simple stone memorial in its quiet setting amid the shedding alders. Here I read the chiseled words that Hemingway himself had written before his death in a eulogy for a friend:

> Best of all he loved the fall
> The leaves yellow on the cottonwoods
> Leaves floating on the trout streams
> And above the hills
> The high blue windless skies . . .
> Now he will be a part of them forever.

After the tranquillity of the memorial site, I prepared myself for the hustle and bustle of Sun Valley. Instead, I found the resort to be much like Ketchum, in a sort of dormant state, waiting to awaken to winter. In Sun Valley I did what a lot of visitors do—I ate. With so many first-class restaurants packed into the relatively small Ketchum/Sun Valley area, I defy anyone to resist temptation and return to their rig's galley.

Since many of the restaurants in Sun Valley are open for dinner only, I returned to Ketchum for lunch at Louie's, a very reasonably priced Italian restaurant that is a local institution. Later, I decided to forego the continental fare at the Lodge Dining Room in the Sun Valley Lodge, primarily because of my earlier meal in Ketchum, but also because the prices are a bit steep. For those whose wallets can stand the strain, I was told the food is excellent. Instead, I was lucky enough to be able to join some local residents in the rustic atmosphere of the Trail Creek Cabin, a local landmark that was a favorite hangout of Hemingway and his pal, Gary Cooper. The food, by the way—good old American Western style—was excellent. (The restaurant is open only in the winter.)

Besides restaurants, and skiing, of course, Sun Valley has a lot more to offer. In fact, there are plenty of activities to keep anyone busy at just about any time of the year: hiking along a myriad of nearby trails, ice skating year round, a number of tennis courts and golf courses, balloon trips, rafting tours, art classes, and spectator activities such as semipro hockey during the winter season and live theater at the rustically styled Sun Valley Opera House. And no one coming to Sun Valley should miss one of the daily showings of the classic Sonja Henie film, *Sun Valley Serenade.*

After a couple of days of relaxation around Sun Valley, I decided it was time to start working off the extra calories by getting back to a

Sun Valley.
The rustic charms of Sun Valley invite the visitor to linger here.

less sedentary life-style. Back on SR 75 I drove out of Ketchum, south about 10 miles, to the small town of Hailey. Much less famous than its neighboring communities, Hailey is no less interesting. Like Idaho City at the other end of the Sawtooth Loop, Hailey at one time played a key role in the early development of Idaho. It was the center for the Mineral Hill mining district and an important rail center with the arrival of the railroad in May of 1883.

Though it has also diminished in size, a lot of Hailey's early charm remains in several old Victorian structures still standing at various points around town. The Blaine County Historical Museum is housed in one of these old brick buildings at the corner of North Main and Galena. On First Avenue there is the three-story Blaine County Courthouse, built in 1883, and on Second Avenue South, at the northeast corner, a 1½-story, unassuming frame building, the birthplace of of Hailey's most famous son, poet Ezra Pound, is still standing.

Motoring south from Hailey, I quickly left the spectacular scenery of the Sawtooth valley behind as the country turned once again to high desert terrain. But here the lack of scenery didn't bother me because I was more interested in stopping off near the town of Bellevue to try

Hemingway Country.
Visitors can walk the quiet path alongside Trail Creek to reach the simple stone memorial to Ernest Hemingway.

my luck fly fishing on Silver Creek. As it turned out, my luck wasn't very good—I think all that rich food in Sun Valley slowed down my casting arm. However, I have been told that Silver Creek is one of the best dry fly streams in the United States. I'll be back.

South of Bellevue, before reaching I-84, are a couple of other points of interest. About 20 miles south of town, travelers may visit the Shoshone Ice Cave, a natural formation discovered in 1880 that was used to produce and store ice for the nearby town of Shoshone. In the 1930s the WPA built a second entrance to the cave, which, as one Shoshone resident observed, promptly made the ice "melt faster than

Craters of the Moon

About 40 miles east of the junction of SR 75 and US 20, travelers will find the stark world of Craters of the Moon National Monument. The basaltic lava fields of this strange landscape cover 83 square miles, much of which can be seen from the comfort of your rig on a driving tour through the site.

hog fat in a hot skillet." Since that time the proper air current circulation has been restored to the cave and ice formation has been reestablished. At the entrance to the cave is a display of prehistoric animal fossils excavated from the interior. A few miles further south of this cave, the traveler encounters Mammoth Cave, a quarter-mile-long lava tube discovered in 1902. Near the cave entrance an A-frame visitor center houses more than 400 stuffed birds, one of the largest collections of avian taxidermy in the nation.

Nearing the junction with I-84 and the end of the Sawtooth Loop, I reflected on the remarkable diversity of this relatively small region. In just a few days I had left Boise, traveled back into Idaho's history, explored one of the state's most scenic backroad routes, and many areas that, until recently, were so remote they were cut off from modern communication. And, finally, I had visited one of the world's most famous jet-set resorts. All in all, a rare and remarkable journey.

POINTS OF INTEREST: Idaho Tour 1

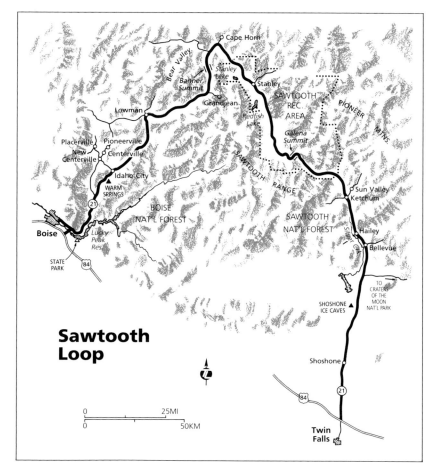

Sawtooth Loop

P.M., Sunday 1 P.M. to 4 P.M., June 1 to September 15.

Placerville: *Henrietta Penrod Museum.* Usually open from June 1 to mid-September. Inquire in Idaho City for hours and fees.

Ketchum: *Sun Valley Center for Arts and Humanities.* In Walnut Avenue Mall; open year-round, featuring lectures, concerts, art classes, and other special events. Fees vary. (208) 726-9491.

Hailey: *Blaine County Historical Museum,* North Main Street. Wednesday to Monday, 10 A.M. to 5 P.M., June 15 to September 15. Adults 50 cents, children under 12, free.

OUTFITTERS
Big Wood Ski Tours, P.O. Box 1469, Ketchum, Idaho 83340.

Busterback Ranch Nordic Touring Center, Star Route, Ketchum, Idaho 83340, (208) 774-2217.

Middle Fork River Company, P.O. Box 233, Sun Valley, Idaho 83353

Middle Fork River Expeditions, P.O. Box 199, Stanley, Idaho 83278, (208) 774-3659.

Rocky Mountain River Tours, Middle Fork; P.O. Box 2252, Boise, Idaho 83701, (208) 344-6668.

Sawtooth Sleighs, Sawtooth National Recreation Building, Ketchum, Idaho 83440 (208) 726-9449.

Silver Creek Outfitters, P.O. Box 418, Ketchum, Idaho 83440, (208) 726-5282.

RESTAURANTS
Ketchum: *Kneadery,* 260 Leadville Avenue North (208) 726-9462 (American). *Louie's Pizza and Italian Restaurant,* 331 Leadville Avenue North, (208) 726-7775 (a Ketchum institution offering excellent Italian-American food at reasonable prices).

Sun Valley: *Lodge Dining Room,* Sun Valley Lodge, (208) 622-4111, ext. 2150 (continental cuisine, expensive).

ACCESS: From *I-84,* eight miles east of Boise, take *SR 21* north; in Boise, take *Main Street* which becomes *Warm Springs Avenue* east to junction of *SR 21.* To reverse tour as outlined, *exit I-84* at Twin Falls and take *SR 75* north.

INFORMATION: *Boise Basin Chamber of Commerce,* Main St. and Hwy. 21, Box 70, Idaho City, Idaho 83631, (208) 392-4290; *Sun Valley-Ketchum . Chamber of Commerce,* 8th and Main, Ketchum, or P. O. Box 2420, Sun Valley, Idaho 83353, (208) 726-4471, (800) 634-3397.

ANNUAL EVENTS:
Idaho City: *Arts and Crafts Festival,* last weekend in June.

Stanley: *Busterback Stampede* (cross-country ski race), February; *Sawtooth Derby,* March; *Whitewater Rodeo* (kayak slalom race), June.

Ketchum: *Wagon Days,* Labor Day Weekend.

Bellevue: *Labor Day Festival.*

Sun Valley: *Christmas Eve Torchlight Parade and Caroling.*

MUSEUMS AND GALLERIES:
Idaho City: *Idaho City Museum,* Montgomery Street at Wall Street. Monday to Saturday, 11 A.M. to 4

The Payette River Scenic Route

The river nobly foams and flows,
The charm of this enchanted ground,
And all its thousand turns disclose
Some fresher beauty varying round....

Lord Byron, *Childe Harold's Pilgrimage*

W ithin the first five miles of Idaho's State Route 55, just north of Boise, I kept looking for a spot to turn around. Judging by the scenery—empty, rolling, brown hills—I was sure I had made a mistake choosing this route. And if that wasn't disappointment enough, manuevering a 35-foot motorhome around the sharp curves and over the bumpy road surface seemed like an ordeal I could do without.

But like a lot of southwest Idaho, traveling SR 55 requires some patience. Just about the time it seems certain you are headed into a vast wasteland, you round a curve and find a spectacular vista of snowcapped mountain peaks and lush green forests unfolding in front of you.

Then, of course, there is the road. This particular section of SR 55—officially designated the Payette River Scenic Route by the state—begins as a pothole-pocked, narrow, bumpy road just north of Boise (repairs may have been made by now), then smooths out about the same time it begins its winding course northward along the banks of the North Fork of the Payette River. In the process the road cuts deep into what can only be characterized as an RVers' paradise.

Along the Payette route something beckons for every RVer. For hunters there are open fields, deep forests, and inviting lakes for migrating ducks and geese. Those same lakes, of course, invite anglers, who will find some of the best bass fishing in the Northwest. For those who like the challenge of fly fishing, the rivers and streams that lace the landscape here offer some excellent trout fishing. Hikers and backpackers can explore a number of trails winding back into the Boise National Forest. And those who just want to simply take it easy may enjoy spectacular views in just about any direction they look from their campsites.

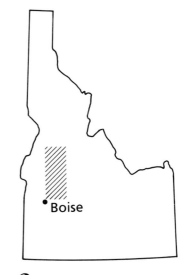

Tour *2* 156 miles

Side trip to Yellow Pine and Stibnite, 106 miles

BOISE • HORSESHOE BEND • BANKS • CASCADE • HORSETHIEF BASIN • CASCADE LAKE • DONNELLY • ROSEBERRY • MCCALL • PONDEROSA STATE PARK

Out from the Boise Basin

None of that, however, was readily apparent as I pointed the motorhome north and began the climb out of the Boise Basin to the Payette River valley. For about 20 miles, as it twisted and turned in its gradual ascent, the road cut through rolling hills dotted with high desert chaparral. Then, as I crested a small summit outside of the small town of Horseshoe Bend, the desert brown turned abruptly to mountain green.

The Payette River

Just north of town I crossed the North Fork of the Payette for the first time. As the road snaked along the banks of the river, I found the going slow, at times because of SR 55's narrow, sharp turns, but mainly be-

Payette takes its name from Frances Payette, a Hudson's Bay trapper.

Horsethief Basin.
Although the origins of the area's name have been lost in the past, residents believe the basin was a hiding spot for stolen horses at one time.

cause the scenery here is so distracting. For about 40 miles, from Horseshoe Bend north to Cascade, the North Fork of the Payette tumbles rapidly—at one point 1,700 feet in just 15 miles—through the lush green canyon bordered by pine-covered slopes.

Since this is one of the most popular white water stretches in all of Idaho, in the summer you're sure to spot kayakers and rafters pitting their skills against the churning waters. For the initiated, the river is filled with Class III rollers, reversals, and riffles. Two of the last rapids on the river are appropriately named Climax and AMF—"Adios My Friend."

Unfortunately, the river's future as a major recreation area appears to be in doubt. Idaho Power Company was granted a license in 1982 to establish a hydroelectric project along this stretch of river. The ambitious, $220 million project will establish at least two diversion dams along the North Fork of the Payette, as well as three generating units just north of Banks.

For now, though, the scenery and the river remain unspoiled, and the drive from Horseshoe Bend, through Banks and up to Cascade is one of the most scenic in the state. About 10 miles south of Cascade

"That which is best left alone is not always what least allures." (Some residents feel that Idaho Power is a bit like the little girl who said she knew how to spell banana, *but just didn't know when to stop.)*

Cascade–Arrowhead Campground
Located in a tranquil, wooded setting, this is a perfect stopover site. In summer, one could actually cast a line from the door of the rig.

Cascade from the Air.
The town of Cascade is nestled in the beautiful Long Valley, on the shores of Cascade Lake.

that scenery changes abruptly as SR 55 breaks out into the lovely Long Valley, then races straight toward the horizon, cutting through green ranchlands dotted with peacefully grazing cattle.

Nestled in this beautiful valley, on the shores of deep blue Cascade Lake, I found the town of Cascade (the rapids in the river suggested the name) to be the perfect base for exploring the area, and Arrowhead Campground at the south edge of town the best place in the area for a few days' stopover. Located in a pleasant wooded setting on the banks of the Payette, the campground offers some riverside campsites that allow you actually to cast a line from the door of your rig.

Cascade Lake

The campground is also a short drive from Cascade Lake, a 20-mile-long, 4½-mile-wide reservoir said to be the most productive man-made lake in Idaho. Anglers catch more than 400,000 perch, coho salmon, rainbow, and brown trout here each year. Boats are available for rent, and boat ramps are easily accessible in areas large enough to maneuver an RV. For those who prefer to keep their feet on dry land, the fishing from the shore is also reported to be excellent.

When I turned in the first night in Cascade, it was with the intention of trying my luck the next morning. At dawn, however, I found a premature, late September snowstorm had dumped about four inches of fresh white powder on the valley overnight. Although the snow was all that was needed to turn the countryside into a Christmas card, it, and temperatures hovering in the high 30s, made fishing on the lake, no matter how promising, an activity that was best postponed.

Fortunately, the roads remained passable, and residents assured me the snow would be gone by midday. So instead of heading for the lake I decided to do some exploring along some of valley's backroads. I was particularly interested in the Warm Lake Road that heads east from town past the turnoff to Horsethief Basin and ultimately to Warm Lake.

On to Horsethief Basin

In a region so rich with recreation opportunities, Horsethief Basin is another area seemingly made just for RVers. The origins of the basin's name have been lost in history, but residents believe the basin was at one time a popular spot with thieves who found the hilly terrain the perfect hiding place for stolen horses.

Today the basin still harbors livestock: cattle from the surrounding ranches that graze the open slopes. It is also an active logging area, but RVers are welcome to explore the network of well-maintained dirt roads that link a number of small lakes nestled among pine groves. Camping is permitted in several unimproved campgrounds, most of which are situated on the shores of the lakes. A few words of warning: During the summer, the months of peak activity, keep a wary eye out for fast-moving logging trucks.

The Warm Lake Resort Area

From Horsethief Basin I returned to the Warm Lake Road and headed east once again, driving about 25 miles along a road lined with thick stands of lodgepole pine, over a small summit, and then dropping down into the Warm Lake resort area. Named for a warm spring that empties into the south side of the lake, Warm Lake also has the reputation of offering excellent fishing for both rainbow and brown trout. Unfortunately, the only overnight accommodations here are the cabins of the Warm Lake Lodge. For RVers the lake is a day-use area only.

For most RVers Warm Lake is also going to be the turnaround point for the return drive to Cascade. For those who have a strong spirit of adventure and a rig that can take the abuse, an alternative tour cuts into the rugged backcountry over roads that, as one local put it, "have more curves than a case of mule shoes."

Besides the rough roads, the real obstacle along this route is the Elk Creek Summit (8,670 feet), which can be closed by snow until midsummer. Before attempting the drive, call the National Forest Service office in McCall to find out the condition of the pass.

Two Backroad Choices

If the pass is open and you've decided to give it a try, you have a choice of two routes out of Warm Lake. One is a 50-mile drive down the South Fork-Poverty Flat Road, and the other is a 35-mile trip east and north along Johnson Creek on the Landmark Road. Both routes are exceptionally scenic and and eventually take you to the historic, decaying villages of Yellow Pine and Stibnite, the sites of mining activity in the early 1900s. Although gold ($21 million worth was taken over a 20-year period) first lured miners to the area, rich deposits of other minerals—antimony, silver, mercury, and tungsten—were discovered

Old West Panorama.
RVers may unexpectedly come upon riders and dogs tending their herds of cattle as they travel the backroads of Idaho.

and mined until the deposits began to play out in the late 1950s. When the last residents left here in 1959, many of them had their homes trucked out with them.

If you continue north at the road that junctions with the Yellow Pine-Stibnite route, you will come to a marker along the side of the road that is a memorial to an early prospector, Profile Sam Wilson. Legend has it that Profile Sam had a number of secret mines in the area which he worked until, depressed by the hardscrabble life of a sourdough miner, he committed suicide in 1935. His friends buried him in Yellow Pine and erected the memorial on what is now known as Profile Summit.

A Visit to the Cascade Area

Having survived this backcountry detour, you'll want to return to Cascade—perhaps for a tour of the Boise-Cascade lumber mill. At the time of my visit, activity was severely curtailed because of both the time of the year and the fact that Idaho's lumber industry has been hard hit economically in recent years. But this mill, one of the few that remains in the area, is still in operation and open for guided tours.

Donnelly

As promised, the snow had melted by the time I returned to Cascade that afternoon, but the weatherman offered little hope for temperatures that would make a day on the lake comfortable. So the next morning I headed north on SR 55 for 15 miles to the hamlet of Donnelly. The youngest town in the valley, Donnelly was founded in 1930 as a lumber town and the headquarters for the Richmond and Samuel Pea Company. During the '30s, as migrant workers flocked to the pea plant and loggers were drawn by the lumber mill, the population of this little town grew to respectable numbers. Old-timers who remember those days say Saturday nights in Donnelly's dance hall were a raucous occasion.

Since the lumberjacks moved on and the pea company shut down during World War II, Donnelly has declined but refuses to die. All that are left now are two restaurants and a tavern, a small general store, and an art gallery.

Roseberry

Roseberry's Methodist Church was opened to any denomination that requested permission to hold services; the sexton used to say "We're all spittin' at the same crack."

Speaking of history, a sign at the south edge of town directs travelers 1½ miles to the east to Roseberry, a town that declined after the railroad was routed through Donnelly. Technically a ghost town, Roseberry now consists of just three buildings, all clustered at an intersection of two county roads. The fading white, paint-flaked buildings, one of which is the old Roseberry Methodist church, are exceptionally photogenic, especially in the early morning hours. On

Ghost Town Church.
The old Roseberry Methodist Church contains the Valley County Museum and is open to visitors.

weekend afternoons during the summer the church, which contains the Valley County Museum, stocked with artifacts of local interest, is open to visitors.

Instead of backtracking from Roseberry to Donnelly and SR 55, I decided to take the parallel county road north as far as it would lead. As it turned out, it didn't lead me very far. Just two miles up the road I found myself in the middle of an Old West cattle drive. I pulled the motorhome to a stop as two riders on horseback, accompanied by a frantically working dog, guided their small herd down the middle of the road. Just as I stopped, the cattle got their first look at the motorhome and immediately turned and headed back toward the riders. Not even the barking dog could turn them.

One of the riders, who turned out to be an attractive young woman bundled against the cold in heavy mackinaw, yelled for me to cut the engine. As I turned the key and the engine died, the riders and dog

Roseberry.
This photogenic ghost town boasts a total of three buildings, all clustered at the crossing of two country roads.

went to work to turn the herd. Like poetry in motion, they cut back and forth behind the herd, riding across the road and down into the gullies on either side, rounding up straying cattle and finally getting the lead steer to move past the motorhome. As the young woman rode by I offered my apologies, and in return got a smile and a wave—a typically friendly gesture of Idaho hospitality.

Although the riders didn't seem disturbed by my intrusion into the cattle drive, I decided it might be best to return to the main highway. A couple of miles up the road I turned left back to SR 55, then turned north for the remaining 15 miles to McCall.

McCall and Ponderosa State Park

As one of Idaho's better-known resort areas, McCall can attract a lot of travelers during the summer months, but the town still does not get the crush of tourists that descend on the Ketchum-Sun Valley area. It's hard to understand why, since it offers an ideal summer climate, a beautiful setting on the shores of Payette Lake, one of the best state parks in all of Idaho, and some exceptional events.

Cattle Crossing.
The author found himself in the middle of an Old West cattle drive outside of
Roseberry.

McCall was founded in 1891 by Tom McCall, an early settler who
purchased squatter's rights to the site for a team and wagon. The town
grew as a lumber center when Warren Gold Dredge Company built a
sawmill on the shores of Payette Lake. The enterprising Tom McCall
soon purchased the mill and used the lumber produced there to build
the first structures in the town. Although the original mill was later de-
stroyed by a fire, others were constructed in its place, including the
last mill operated by Boise-Cascade that closed in 1977.

Tourism got its start in McCall around the turn of the century when
one of the residents, Anneas "Jews Harp Jack" Wyatte, began running
an excursion boat on the lake during the summer months. When the
railroad arrived a few years later, McCall became a full-fledged summer
retreat, especially popular with residents of Boise.

Today attempts are being made to further McCall's development as a
summer resort, with the building of a number of vacation condomin-
iums on the east side of town. All in all, though, McCall retains its
charm as a quiet mountain retreat.

For RVers the best way to fully enjoy McCall's pleasures is first to
settle in at Ponderosa State Park at the north edge of town. Open year

Sawmill at McCall.
The town of McCall was originally founded when Tom McCall purchased the sawmill built by Warren Gold Dredge Company on the shores of Lake Payette; he used the lumber produced here to build the town's first structures.

round, but limited to day use during the winter, the 1,280-acre heavily wooded park is located on a peninsula that juts out into Payette Lake. Campsites number 170, two-thirds of which have water and electricity.

Campers in Ponderosa have an extensive network of trails and roads that let them explore virtually every corner of the park. One evening, just before sunset, I took the road that leads up to a promontory overlooking the north end of the lake, a vantage point that gave me a spectacular view of the sun dropping over the lake and the lights of McCall coming to life in the distance.

The park also has an abundance of wildlife, and on more than one night deer grazed quietly through the campground in the evening. And, of course, situated on the shores of Payette Lake, the park is an excellent base for anglers who can either fish from the shore or rent a boat from the resident concessionaire.

Although Ponderosa qualifies as a paradise for photographers, one of the main attractions of the area for photo buffs is the old decaying lumber mill that sits on the eastern lake shore. In the morning, when the mists are rising off the waters, the mill becomes the focal point for a soft, moody shot of the lake. In the evening, as the mill catches the last rays of the setting sun, the scene changes dramatically. Even if you're not a dedicated photographer, it's an ideal photo opportunity.

For those looking for more than scenery, McCall has three special events held at various times of the year, as well as a fascinating tour of the U.S. Forest Service Smokejumper Headquarters that was established here in 1943. The base for the parachuting firefighters who battle forest fires throughout the West is located on Mission Street across from the McCall-Donnelly School. During the summer, tours are given every day between 9 A.M. and 6 P.M. For reservations, phone (208) 634-8151.

As for the special events, if you are in the area on the Fourth of July, you will be able to take in the town's celebration that includes a waterfront boat parade and fireworks over the lake. On Labor Day, weekend antique car enthusiasts hold their annual parade through town in a variety of vintage automobiles. And on the first weekend in February, whimsical and intricate ice sculptures line the streets of McCall as part

McCall.
Situated on the shores of Lake Payette, McCall boasts some of the state's best parks and an ideal summer climate.

In 1938 McCall and Payette Lake served as the locale for the MGM film Northwest Passage, *starring Spencer Tracy, Robert Young, and Walter Brennan.*

of the town's Winter Carnival celebration. One important note: Those planning to attend the carnival should be forewarned that they will probably find more than ice sculptures on the streets of McCall in February. With an average annual snowfall of about 151 inches, McCall has the distinction of having the highest mean annual snowfall of any town in the state.

All that snow, however, shouldn't deter travel to McCall or any of the other destinations in this tour. The blanket of white may restrict access to some points of interest but, like the early snowfall that greeted my visit here, it only enhances others. One of the special aspects of this tour is that SR 55 remains open all year. With many of the campgrounds in the area also offering year round accommodations, RVers have four-season access to the Payette River Scenic Route. Don't miss it.

POINTS OF INTEREST: Idaho Tour 2

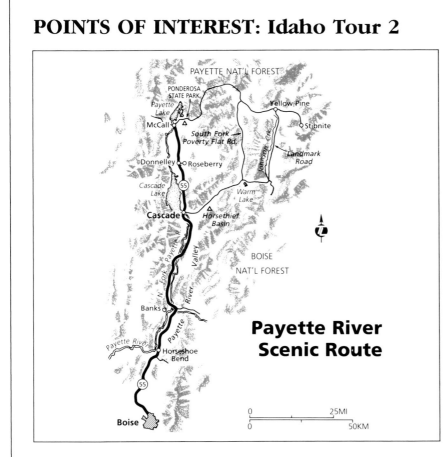

Payette River Scenic Route

0   25MI
0   50KM

ACCESS: From *I-84* at Boise, north on *SR 55.*

INFORMATION: *Cascade Chamber of Commerce,* 112 Main St., Cascade, Idaho 83611, (208) 382-4921; *McCall Chamber of Commerce,* Third St. and Polk, Box D, McCall, Idaho 83638, (208) 634-7631.

ANNUAL EVENTS:
Cascade: *Winter Jamboree,* February; *Thunder Mountain Days,* (Western celebration, barbecue), July 4.

McCall: *Winter Carnival,* February; *Fourth of July Celebration* (fireworks over lake); *Folklore Society Annual Folk Festival,* July; *Tour of Homes* August; *BBQ and Antique Car Show,* September.

MUSEUMS AND GALLERIES:
Roseberry: *Valley County Museum,* generally open weekends 1 P.M. to 5 P.M. during summer months, free. (208) 325-8839.

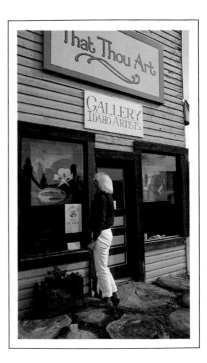

SPECIAL ATTRACTIONS:
Cascade: *Boise-Cascade Mill.* Open year-round for 45-minute guided tours, free. Appointments recommended, (208) 382-4241.

McCall: *Smokejumper Headquarters.* Tours of U.S. Forest Service's firefighting facilities. Open during summer months, 9 A.M. to 6 P.M., reservations required. Payette National Forest, P. O. Box 1026, McCall, Idaho 83638, (208) 634-8151.

OUTFITTERS:
Epley's Idaho Outdoor Adventures, 1107 N. Davis, Box 987, McCall, Idaho 83638, (208) 634-5173.

RESTAURANTS:
McCall: *Shore Lodge,* on U.S. 95 and SR 55 loop, on shores of Payette Lake, (208) 634-2244 (American, features outdoor dining in summer on terrace overlooking lake).

Southwest Idaho

They say there is a land,
  Where crystal waters flow,
O'er beds of quartz and purest gold,
  Way out in Idaho.

We'll need no pick or spade,
  No shovel, pan, or hoe;
The largest chunks are 'top of ground,
  Way out in Idaho.

Frank French, *Idaho*

"**V**oyez le bois!" That exclamation, loosely translated as "look at all those trees," is what the early French explorers are said to have shouted when they got their first glimpse of the Boise Basin in 1811. One hundred and seventy-five years later when I came into Boise and put down temporary roots at the Fiesta Park campground west of town, I realized that, like those early explorers, I had stumbled onto something special. So special, in fact, that state tourism officials have dubbed this region of Idaho *Treasureland.*

Boise—An Oasis in the Desert

Indeed it must have seemed a treasureland to the Frenchmen too, after weeks of trekking across the arid wilderness of the Snake River plain, to suddenly find an oasis of green fed by the cool blue waters of the river that now bears the city's name. A few years later, Boise was an important outpost along the Oregon Trail, and by 1862, at the height of Idaho's gold rush, it was well on its way to becoming one of the most important cities in the Northwest.

Today Boise (pronounced boy-see) is still an oasis in the high desert terrain of southwest Idaho, an oasis both geographically and culturally. A generally favorable summertime climate—warm days, low humidity, and cool nights— makes Boise not only the perfect RV vacation spot, but an ideal summer haven for snowbirds. Beyond that, though, Boise's attractions lie in the myriad offerings of the city itself as well as its position as the hub of a backroad tour of some of southwest Idaho's most scenic and historically interesting locales.

Although, with a population of 110,000 and growing importance as a center of commerce, Boise definitely qualifies as a city, it hasn't lost any of its small-town, Western hospitality. At the same time, it boasts a sophistication not found in cities five times its size. There are literally unlimited things to see and do in Boise.

A City of Trees

With some 16,000 acres of parks within the city limits, Boise remains a "City of Trees." In the summertime especially, a lot of activities center around the park areas which, taken together, form the Boise River Greenbelt, stretching for 10 miles through the center of town. Here, in addition to the usual park activities such as tennis, archery, horseshoes, and golf, are more than eight miles of riverside paths for walking, jogging, or bicycling. The greenbelt also is home to a zoo, the very impressive Boise Gallery of Art, the Idaho Historical Museum, and the recently completed Morrison Center for the Performing Arts, a first-

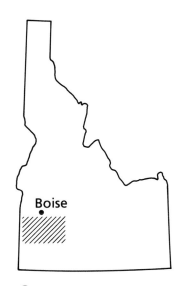

Tour 3 *134 miles*

BOISE • NAMPA • CALDWELL • DEER FLAT NATIONAL WILDLIFE REFUGE • LAKE LOWELL • SNAKE RIVER BIRDS OF PREY AREA • SILVER CITY • BRUNEAU • HAMMETT • THREE ISLAND CROSSING STATE PARK • GLENNS FERRY

Depot Hill.
Union Pacific Depot is an excellent spot for a downtown view of Boise.

Riverfront Park.
The Boise River offers many recreational activities, including "tubing"—cruising by tube or raft.

rate facility with a packed schedule of theater and concert performances. Finally, the annual Shakespeare Festival held throughout the summer on the green at One Capitol Center draws enthusiastic crowds.

Floating the Boise

The real summertime fun here, though, is floating the Boise River past the lush, tree-lined banks of the greenbelt. "Tubing on the Boise" is said to be one of the favorite pastimes of Boiseans and is so popular that a special day, called the Super Float, is now held each year in early August. On that day as many as 15,000 residents of the city may get together to make the six-mile, two-hour float from Barber Park to Ann Morrison Park.

Unfortunately, I missed the big day, but in late August, the weather was still warm enough to encourage a trip down the river. For those who want to try it, all you do is park your rig at Ann Morrison Park and take the "tubers shuttle" (operates 11 A.M. to 6 P.M. weekdays, 11 A.M. to 7 P.M. weekends) for the 15-minute drive to Barber Park. Before leaving, you can rent a tube at the park ($2.00 for the day), or wait until you get to Barber Park to pick up your tube. If you want a little more protection from the chilly (60°) water, rafts are also available.

By tube or raft—I opted for the tube—floating the Boise is one of the most enjoyable and relaxing experiences you will have during your stay in the city. The stretch of river that runs past the greenbelt is carefully maintained to assure that it is clear of snags. For the most part, the surface of the river is glassy, although three gentle stretches of rapids liven up the trip, so you drift at a lazy pace that allows you to take in the postcard-perfect scenery. As beautiful as it is in summer, residents told me that drifting the river on a warm Indian summer day in mid to late September can be a breathtaking experience when the river's banks are ablaze with fall colors. At that time of year, when the air temperature sometimes falls well below the temperature of the water, you would definitely want to go by raft and team up with a fellow RVer for transportation, since the shuttle bus is not in service in that season.

Tootin Tater.
The Boise Tour Train, better known as the *Tootin Tater,* is an excellent way to see the sights of Boise while the guide entertains with a humorous monologue. (*Boise Convention and Visitors Bureau*)

The Boise Tour Train—"Tootin Tater"

In the fall the Boise Tour Train also ceases operation, but from the first of June until Labor Day it is probably the best way for RVers to take in the sights of downtown Boise. The train, called the *Tootin Tater*, is a whimsical replica of an 1890s puffer belly engine. Driven by a jovial tour guide the train with its three open-air cars departs at various times of the day from in front of the Historical Museum in Julia Davis Park. As it winds through the city streets, the guide notes points of interest and relates historic and contemporary facts about the city. It's an interesting tour and a good way to get a quick glimpse of Boise's past and present. What makes it special fun, though, is the guide himself. His narrative is laced with anecdotes and a heavy emphasis on puns that focus on Idaho's fame as the potato growing capital of the country—"Why wouldn't King Russet Potato let his daughter meet Walter Cronkite? Because he was just a commentater."

During the tour, between the laughter and the groans, two points of interest—the Capitol Building and the Eighth Street Markeplace—piqued my interest. After returning to the park at the end of the tour, I drove my motorhome into downtown Boise and found a large lot off Ninth Street that could accommodate RVs. From there, it was just a short walk to both the capitol and the marketplace.

VIP.
"Famous," mascot of the Boise Convention and Visitors Bureau, is known in town as a VIP—Very Important Potato! (*Boise Convention and Visitors Bureau*)

The Capitol Building

From the outside the capitol, completed in 1920, looks pretty much like a lot of other state capitol buildings, although it is distinguished by the fact that it is beautifully landscaped and was designed to be a replica of the national capitol in Washington, D.C. Inside, however, I found a number of interesting historical and agricultural exhibits. I also found

Idaho Capitol.
The capitol building in Boise was designed as a replica of our nation's capitol in Washington, D.C.

The first and second sessions of the Territorial legislature were held in Lewiston, the trading outpost of Walla Walla, in December, 1863, and November, 1864. On the agenda was the decision on where the Territorial capital would be located. Before the debate could even begin, a delegation (from Boise, of course) stole the seal and legislative records and ran off with them to Boise City where a frame building was designated as the seat of Idaho Territory. Here the capital remains to this day.

the state tourism office, located just off the rotunda, well stocked with books and brochures on various sites and events, providing the traveler with the latest information on the state.

The Marketplace

After strolling through the capitol, I walked back to the Eighth Street Marketplace, a quaint and colorful complex of shops and restaurants housed in what was formerly Boise's warehouse district. Opened a few years ago, more and more shops are being added as the marketplace grows in popularity with residents and tourists alike. Wine connoisseurs—and just plain wine lovers—will find the cellar store of the Ste. Chappelle Winery, Idaho's largest wine producer, a particularly interesting stop. A relatively new winery, producing since 1977, it has earned praise from wine experts and won a number of prizes. You can sample several varieties in the wine-tasting room. I particularly enjoyed the 1983 Johannisberg Riesling and the 1981 Chardonnay Reserve.

Union Pacific Depot and Depot Hill

After spending a few hours wandering through the quaint old structures of the busy marketplace, I retrieved the motorhome and drove south on Capitol Boulevard, crossing the river and climbing to the site of the old Union Pacific Depot that sits atop a hill overlooking the greenbelt and downtown Boise. For a view of the city, the depot is an unsurpassed vantage point, but the area, known as Depot Hill, is interesting in itself.

Union Depot—First Day.
A crowd of people at Union Pacific Depot on its opening day welcome the first mainline train on April 16, 1925. (*Idaho State Historical Society*)

The depot, built in 1925 in Spanish Colonial-style architecture, looks as if it would be more at home in the Southwest than here in Idaho's largest city. The front is a broad expanse of sloping lawn and the well-groomed Platt Gardens filled with green shrubbery and, at the time, early fall blossoms. The beautifully manicured lawn and gardens, which are officially part of the Boise park system and owned by the city, are maintained by the Union Pacific Railroad.

The Old Idaho Penitentiary and Environs

After watching the shadows of the sunset fall across the city, I drove back to the campground to map out a final day's tour in Boise. Reading through the brochures collected at the capitol, I realized I had only scratched the surface of the city's attractions. But a choice had to be made, so I decided the Old Idaho Penitentiary, billed as the "most fascinating tourist attraction in the city and, aside from Alcatraz, the most informative prison tour in the West" was something I couldn't miss.

In the morning, with the sun hidden behind a heavy layer of overcast and hint of early fall chill in the air, it seemed as if I had picked a fitting day to visit the prison. To get there I retraced part of the previous day's route, turning off Capitol Boulevard on to Main Street and following it until it became Warm Springs Avenue on the eastern side of the city. I deliberately selected this route to the prison site because

Boise Residence.
Warm Springs Avenue is lined with elegant old homes. The waters from the geothermal deposit they sat upon were used for heating.

I was told it was one of the most interesting routes in the city.

Lined with stately old homes, Warm Springs Avenue remains one of Boise's most prestigious neighborhoods. Although the homes are beautiful examples of turn-of-the-century architecture and many are historically significant, the most interesting fact about this eight-block area is that it sits atop a geothermal deposit whose waters flow at 170°F. In 1890 a well was developed at the eastern edge of the street which allowed the waters to be used to heat the residences along the avenue. Today some two hundred homes are still heated by the nine miles of pipe connected to the well.

At the end of Warm Springs Avenue, a left turn onto Penitentiary Road took me into the long driveway leading to the prison grounds. After parking off the side of the drive I walked past a high turret, alongside the massive gray stone walls to the tree-shaded entrance. The green, park-like setting which makes up the grounds is not only a sharp contrast to the gray exterior of the prison, it is also markedly different from the generally colorless interior.

Completed in 1872 with convict labor and in use as late as 1973, the penitentiary is indeed one of the most interesting attractions in Boise. (No doubt part of the fascination lies in our ability to place ourselves imaginatively as inmates.) When the cornerstone was laid on July 4, 1870, the local paper noted: "A general attendance of every age and sex is requested to view an edifice that may someday be their home—and not even the wisest knows how soon." Today the prison is no longer home for anyone, but the invitation to visit still stands. Self-guided tours are permitted year round, daily from noon to 4 P.M. except holidays. Those tours include a look at the four-tier main cell block, where you can actually enter a cell, as well as views of the punishment block known as "Siberia," Death Row, and the gallows. A slide presentation and displays provide a detailed history of the prison and some of its more colorful inmates.

A prison tour bonus is the Idaho Transportation Museum, also located on the penitentiary grounds and included in the admission price. The museum's exhibits are a thorough representation of the various vehicles—buggies, stagecoaches, and the like—that played an important role in the early history and settlement of the state. Fire equipment buffs will be interested in the beautifully preserved 1903 steam pumper.

Seemingly out of place here is the Bishops' House, a magnificent Queen Anne-style mansion located across the street from the prison entrance. The house, built in 1899, served as the home of Boise's episcopal bishops during the early part of the century. It was originally located in downtown Boise but was moved to the prison site in 1975 after a voluntary community effort rescued it from the wrecker's ball. Legend has it that "Buffalo Bill" Cody stayed in one of the upstairs guest rooms. The house is now owned by the Idaho Historical Society and is opened periodically for public and private functions.

Into Idaho's Wine Country

Perhaps it was the effect of viewing the grim prison, but by the end of my tour of the penitentiary site, I was ready to hit the road for a tour of the wide open spaces to the south. At dawn I pulled out of Boise and headed west on I-84 toward the twin communities of Nampa and Caldwell. My plan was to head south to the Snake River and the Owyhee desert region by taking SR 55 out of the western edge of Nampa. When I stopped to check my map, however, a brochure outlining an agricultural tour near Caldwell dropped out. The opportunity to stock my rig's galley with fresh fruit and produce, as well as take in a tour of the Ste. Chapelle winery, helped me decide on a detour west of Caldwell.

As instructed, I drove west of Caldwell on I-84 to the Notus/Parma exit, then took U.S. 20-26 along the Boise River through the rich valley farmland. (Over, incidentally, increasingly narrow roads. Caution is definitely advised throughout this backroad portion of the tour, especially if you are driving a large motorhome or pulling a sizable trailer.) At Parma I stopped long enough to buy fresh sweet corn and lettuce, then turned south on U.S. 95, crossing the Boise River, passing through the community of Wilder and then crossing the Snake River at Homedale. A few miles beyond, I found myself back at SR 55 heading east toward Marsing. As the road cut back across the Snake, the brochure told me I was in Sunny Slope, a 25,000-acre region of orchards and vineyards. But you don't need a brochure to tell you what grows here; the area is dotted with fruit stands selling fresh peaches, pears, apricots, cherries, plums, grapes, and raspberries. Here the 1,100-acre Symms Fruit Ranch is the largest orchard and fruit-packing operation in the state.

Besides having some of the richest farmland in all of Idaho, the Sunny Slope area is also the heart of Idaho's wine country. The Ste. Chapelle Winery, located east off SR 55, on Lowell Road, was established in Sunny Slope in 1978 after being moved from a nearby location and the octagonal main building is a replica of the Ste. Chapelle (Saints' Chapel) in Paris that once housed the famous Shroud of Turin. The winery currently grows six varieties of grapes and produces eight different wines. Some 60,000 cases of varietal wines are produced each year for sale throughout the United States and in several foreign countries. Tours are offered daily, except holidays.

Deer Flat and Lake Lowell

Back on SR 55, I found it was only about two miles northeast of Lowell Road to the turnoff for the Deer Flat National Wildlife Refuge and Lake Lowell. The refuge, established in 1909, includes the lake and a broad expanse of the Snake River and serves as a major wintering area for ducks and geese of the Pacific Flyway. Fishing for large and smallmouth bass is said to be good in Lake Lowell. The season is April 15 to September 30.

Snake River Birds of Prey Area

The wildlife refuge was an appropriate prelude to the spectacular Snake River Birds of Prey Area, which I reached by linking up with SR 45 from the lake road, then turning north to junction with an easterly route to Kuna. Driving through Kuna, I followed the signs which directed me south on the gravel road that leads to the area. This 483,000-acre preserve, established in 1971 by Interior Secretary Rogers Morton, now contains the densest concentration of raptors—eagles, hawks, falcons, owls, ospreys, and vultures—in the United States. I parked the motorhome at the visitor center, grabbed my binoculars, and walked to the canyon rim where I was dazzled by both the vistas of the river canyon and a flying exhibition as the various birds dipped and soared on the thermal currents rising from the floor of the river canyon. This is another one of the must stops for anyone visiting the Boise area. If at all possible try to visit during the spring nesting season, and figure on seeing the most flying activity from about 8 A.M. to noon and in the early evening hours.

Eagle Preserve.
Conservation efforts have been so successful at the Birds of Prey area that visitors are likely to catch a glimpse of eaglets, such as these, at the site. (*Montana Travel Promotion*)

Side Trip to Silver City

From here I retraced my route back to Kuna, west to SR 45, then south to SR 78, where I set out for the campground at Bruneau Sand Dunes State Park. For the stouthearted who want to give it a try, I should mention that this route offers an interesting side trip to Silver City, renowned as Idaho's most picturesque mining town, and sometimes called the "Queen of Idaho's ghost towns." The hitch is that the road to Silver City, located off SR 78, about 10 miles from the junction of SR 78 and SR 45, is rough and subject to closure in bad weather. I had been told by a gas station attendant in Kuna that the road was definitely not passable by motorhome or by RVers pulling trailers, but that it could be negotiated by automobile. So, those with tow vehicles and motorhome drivers who have access to a car might want to give it a try. Be prepared for slow going, though, over 23 miles of a narrow dirt and gravel road that peaks out at the 6,676-foot New York Summit (named, incidentally, by promoters who sold mining stock to gullible easterners).

The reward for the trip to Silver City is a chance to see some forty historic buildings in various states of rapidly increasing, but picturesque, decay. One of those is the fifty-room Idaho Hotel, built in the 1860s and at one time one of the finest hotels in the Idaho Territory. A museum established in the old two-story schoolhouse and the remains of the *Idaho Avalanche* newspaper office still stand on the same street as the hotel.

On a hillside at the edge of town is the inevitable old cemetery with a number of fading headstones standing precariously at the gravesites. One grave, that of a local photographer, Hiram E. Leslie, buried in

Silver City Masonic Hall.
The Silver City Masonic Hall, built in 1869, is another of the forty or so original buildings remaining in this historic mining town. (*Idaho State Historical Society*)

Historic Trio.
Three picturesque Silver City buildings include (*from left to right*): Getchel's Drug, the Silver Slipper, and the Granite Block. (*Idaho State Historical Society*)

Silver City Splendor.
A closeup look at Stoddard House shows the intricate detailing of what remains of the facade. (*Idaho State Historical Society*)

Silver Slipper.
The old saloon holds memories of former revelries when Silver City was filled with rowdy miners. (*Idaho State Historical Society*)

One grave, that of a local photographer Hiram E. Leslie, buried in 1882, has an interesting legend. As the story goes, Leslie was accused of cattle rustling, but denied the charge. In protesting his innocence, Leslie said, "If I'm guilty, may God strike me dead." Two days later he was struck by lightning and killed.

Bruneau Sands Dune Park

Those who can't make the Silver City trip won't be disappointed by Bruneau Sand Dunes State Park. The area around the park has been called the "Sahara of the West," and one look will tell you why. The 4,800-acre park is part of the vast Owyhee Desert which stretches across southwestern Idaho and spills into northern Nevada. The area's most immediately recognizable attractions are the two huge sand dunes that cover about 600 acres within the park. They are unique in their formation and include the largest single sand dune in North America, some 470 feet high. The crater-like basin between the dunes is probably the result of unusual wind currents created by the dunes themselves.

Since 1952, when a dam was completed nearby on the Snake River, small lakes have begun appearing within the park boundaries near the dunes. Sadly, geologists predict that the lake at the base of the dunes will destabilize the dunes so they will eventually disappear. For now the dunes remain an unusual sight, especially when viewed against the backdrop of a magnificent desert sunset.

The area is rich in both history and wildlife. The Idaho Department of Parks and Recreation maintains a museum within the park that relates some tales of the early pioneers who passed through the area. It also furnishes information on geologic formations, native plants, and animals. The campground here is very nice but has only 16 sites with full hookups. Another drawback: during the summer months it can be very hot; at the time of my late August visit daytime temperatures climbed into the high 90s, with little relief at night. According to the park ranger, the temperatures can go as high as 110°F., and in winter the thermometer has been known to drop as low as -18°F. Clearly, the best time for a visit here is spring and early fall.

In fact, it was the heat that prompted me to move on. After my overnight stop, I lingered a little the next morning to explore the museum and go for a short walk along part of the five-mile hiking trail (you can buy a patch commemorating your trail walk at the museum). As the sun rose, I pointed my rig eastward on SR 78 toward Hammett.

The Glenns Ferry Area

Two miles east of Hammett I found myself back on I-84, paralleling the Snake River, on the outskirts of the town of Glenns Ferry. One of the most historically significant points in all of Idaho, Glenns Ferry and the nearby Three Island State Park were major milestones on the Oregon Trail. The town is named for Gustavus Glenn, an early settler of the area who started a ferry service across the Snake River in 1863. South of town Three Island State Park takes its name from two separate river crossing points used by early travelers on the Oregon Trail.

The first crossing, Three Island Ford, was the only place where the Snake River could be forded without swimming or floating, thanks to a gravel bar that enabled travelers to cross dry shod. The second crossing, one mile upstream, was called Two Island Crossing. Here crossing was more difficult because wagons had to be floated. Men would swim the river carrying ropes; once on the other side they would pull the wagons across. Because many of the early emigrants were confused about the existence of both crossing points, the area became known by one name, Three Island Crossing.

This area, different from the desert wasteland of Bruneau Sand Dunes, also called for an overnight stop in the park campground. At the visitor center and interpretive area I found some well-mounted historical displays that further explained the travails of the emigrants who traveled west on this route. Afterward, I took a self-guided hike along the Wagon Ride Trail that skirts part of the old Oregon Trail. A corral along the Snake River houses American bison and some longhorn cattle, offering the visitor an opportunity to get a close look and photographs of the two animal species that once roamed freely over the open plains of the Old West.

From the park it is only a short drive north to the east-west route of I-84, a sharp contrast to the old Oregon Trail and today's narrow backroads in southwest Idaho. From here, no matter where you go in Idaho you'll not be able to duplicate the unique variety of the southwest corner of the state. Metropolitan culture and colorful Old West history, rich farmlands and desert vistas—it's all here in Treasureland.

Snake River Crossing.
Three Island Ford, near Glenns Ferry, was the first crossing of the Snake River. The spot contained a gravel bar that allowed travelers to cross dry-shod as they traveled the Oregon Trail. (*Idaho State Historical Society*)

POINTS OF INTEREST: Idaho Tour 3

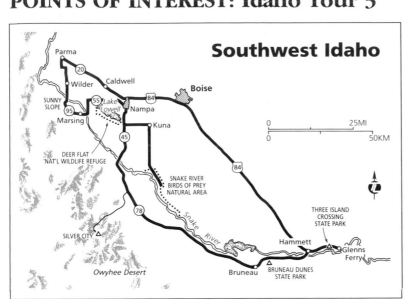

Southwest Idaho

ACCESS: *I-84* at Boise. Eastern part of loop, *I-84* at Glenns Ferry, southwest on *SR 78.*

INFORMATION: *Boise Convention and Visitors Bureau,* Historic Alexander Building, Ninth and Main, Box 2106, Boise, Idaho 83701, (208) 344-7777, (800) 635-5240; *Caldwell Chamber of Commerce,* 300 Frontage St., P.O. Box 819, Caldwell, Idaho 83605, (208) 459-7493; *Glenns Ferry Chamber of Commerce,* Box 317, Glenns Ferry, Idaho 83623, (208) 366-7486; *Mountain Home Chamber of Commerce,* 110 North 3rd St. E., P.O. Box 3, Mountain Home, Idaho 83674, (208) 387-4334.

ANNUAL EVENTS:
Boise: *Birds of Prey Festival,* Mid-May; *Shakespeare Festival,* June through mid-August; *Basque Picnic,* July (street dances); *Art in the Park,* September (arts and crafts festival); *Museum Comes to Life,* September (craft fair, buggy rides); *Basque Carnival and Bazaar,* October; *Traditional Basque Sheepherders Ball,* December (dance and lamb auction).

Caldwell: *Caldwell Night Rodeo,* August.

Glenns Ferry: *Elmore County Fair and Rodeo,* first weekend in August.

Mountain Home: *Basque Sheepherder's Ball,* January; *Air Force Base Open House,* May; *Frontier Days,* first weekend in May; *Air Force Appreciation Days,* first weekend following Labor Day in September.

Nampa: *Snake River Stampede and Festival,* July.

MUSEUMS AND GALLERIES:
Boise: *Boise Art Museum,* 670 South Julia Davis Drive. Monday to Friday 10 A.M. to 5 P.M., Saturday 9 A.M. to 5 P.M., Sunday and holidays 1 P.M. to 5 P.M., donations asked. (208) 345-8330. *Idaho Historical Museum,* at entrance of Julia Davis Park. Monday to Saturday 9 A.M. to 5 P.M., Sunday and holidays 1 P.M. to 5 P.M., free. (208) 334-2120.

Caldwell: *College of Idaho,* 2112 Cleveland Boulevard, Caldwell, 83605, (208) 459-5405. The campus features a number of attractions, including the Glen and Ruth Evans Gem and Mineral Collection, Orma J. Smith Museum of Natural History, David G. Rosenthal Gallery of Arts and Whittenberger Planetarium. Contact campus for information on specific attractions.

Mountain Home: *Elmore County Museum and Historical Foundation,* South Third Street East, Friday and Saturday, 1:30 P.M. to 4 P.M., free. (208)587-8271.

Nampa: *Canyon County Historical Museum,* 1200 Front Street, Tuesday, Thursday, Saturday, 1 P.M. to 5 P.M., Wednesday, 10 A.M. to 4 P.M., free. (208) 467-7611.

SPECIAL ATTRACTIONS:

Boise: *Tootin' Tater Boise Tour Train,* departure at entrance of Julia Davis Park. One-hour guided tours of historic areas, June 1 through Labor Day. Phone (208) 342-4796 for departure times. *Old Idaho Penitentiary,* two-and-a-half miles east on Main Street and Warm Springs Road to Penitentiary Road. Features restored Bishops' House on grounds and Museum of Transportation. Open year-round, daily, noon to 4 P.M., closed holidays. (208) 334-2844. *State Capitol,* Jefferson, West State, 6th and 8th Streets. Monday to Friday, 8 A.M. to 5 P.M., Saturday 9 A.M. to 4 P.M., closed Sunday and holidays, free. (208) 334-2411.

Snake River: *Birds of Prey Natural Area:* This 483,000-acre area has one of world's largest populations of nesting raptors. Center open to visitors at scheduled times throughout week, (208) 362-3716.

Bruneau Sand Dunes: Two sand dunes that cover 600 acres and winter rest haven for thousands of geese, duck, and heron. Park is open to visitors year round, (208) 366-7919.

Nampa: *Swiss Village Cheese Factory,* exit 38 off I-84, at intersection of Star Road and SR 30. Daily, 9 A. M. to 6 P.M., Sunday noon to 4 P.M., free guided tour; reservations required one day in advance. Gift shop and delicatessan. (208) 467-4424.

AGRICULTURE TOURS:

Caldwell: Contact *Caldwell Chamber of Commerce* at address and phone listed previously for maps and information on a 50-mile tour of nearby agricultural areas.

WINERY TOURS:

Caldwell: *Ste. Chapelle Wineries,* off Hwy 55 at Karcher Mall exit, Karcher Road to Lowell Road. Monday to Saturday, 10 A.M. to 6 P.M., Sunday noon to 5 P.M., free. (208) 459-7222. *Weston Winery,* off I-84

at Karcher Road to Sunny Slope area. Monday through Saturday, 11 A.M. to 5 P.M., Sunday 1 P.M. to 5 P.M., free. (208) 454-1682.

OUTFITTERS:
Custom River Tours, P.O. Box 7071, Boise, Idaho 83707, (208) 343-3343.

Cascade River Company, P.O. Box 70, Horseshoe Bend, Idaho 83629, (208) 462-3639.

Whitewater Shop, 9077 West State Street, Boise, Idaho 85703, (208) 342-0750.

Rocky Mountain Fly Shop, 1008 Vista Avenue, Boise, Idaho 83705.

RESTAURANTS:
Boise: *Chart House Restaurant,* 2288 N. Garden Street (American) (208) 336-9370. *Gamekeeper Restaurant,* Owyhee Plaza, 1109 Main Street (continental cuisine, expensive) (208) 343-4611. *Hennessye's,* 802 W. Bannock, (American, moderate to expensive, featuring commanding view of city from atop historic Hoff Building) (208) 342-3505.

Nampa: *Captains HasBrouck House,* 1403 12th Avenue South, (American, dining in restored turn-of-the-century home, moderately priced) (208) 467-7375.

THE GHOSTS OF THE NEZ PERCE NATION
Idaho's Heartland

"Hear me my Chiefs, I am tired;
my heart is sick and sad.
From where the sun now stands,
I will fight no more forever

Chief Joseph's Surrender Speech, October, 5, 1877

I t sounds like a town named in honor of asthma fever sufferers, but in fact, Weiser (pronounced Wee-zer, and named for miner Jacob Weiser who struck gold here in the early 1860s), located in southwest Idaho on U.S. 95 just a few miles north of I-84, is noted more for its music than for its wheezes. Weiser is host each year to the best fiddle players in the world who come here during the third week in June to compete in the National Old-time Fiddlers' Contest and Festival.

An Old-time Fiddle Contest

Although the national competition has only been a tradition in Weiser for little more than twenty years, the festival has roots dating back to the early part of the century when fiddle contests among local musicians were a common event. In 1963, Blaine Stubblefield, then president of the Weiser Chamber of Commerce and a dedicated fiddle aficionado, launched the competition as an annual event. Now each year the annual celebration swells the community of 5,000 to several times that size as people come from all over the country to participate in the festivities. A parade, barbecues, and six full nights of competition and awards for fiddlers, age five to nearly one hundred, keep everyone happy. Impromptu street corner jam sessions lend excitement as fiddlers get together to tune up for the competition.

Gateway to Hell's Canyon

And, of course, there are crowds. For folks who prefer less hectic pursuits and who aren't fans of good old down-home country music, Weiser during festival time is probably a place to avoid. But, for the remaining fifty-one weeks of the year, a visit to Weiser is a decided plus in touring pleasure. Not only is it a historically significant town with some-well preserved examples of Victorian architecture, Weiser also is the gateway to Hell's Canyon and the jumping-off point for an interesting backcountry tour that takes in Idaho's Salmon River canyon and the surrounding country where Chief Joseph and his ill-fated Nez Perce Nation played out their history.

I rolled into Weiser in early fall, long after the lively strains of country music had died away. It was a quiet time of year, perfect for a leisurely look at Weiser's past.

On State Street, I found the old Oregon Short Line Depot, built in 1895, and at 30 East Idaho Street, I found what is probably Weiser's most famous old landmark, the Pythian Castle. The remarkable, dual-turreted meeting hall was built in 1905 by thirty Weiser businessmen who were members of Myrtle Lodge No. 26 of the Order of the

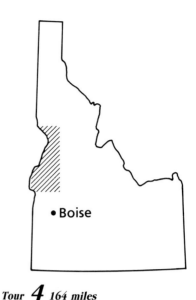

Boise

Tour **4** *164 miles*

WEISER • COUNCIL • HELL'S CANYON • SEVEN DEVILS MOUNTAINS • NEW MEADOWS • KIMBERLAND MEADOWS • ZIM'S HOT SPRINGS • RIGGINS • LUCILE • WHITE BIRD CANYON BATTLEFIELD

Old-time Fiddlers' Contest.
Benny Thomasson is shown playing his fiddle at the National Old-time Fiddlers' Contest in 1980. (*The Idaho Statesman*)

Hell's Canyon.
The Snake River carved this magnificent canyon, in combination with volcanic activity, massive uplifts of the earth, and millions of years of erosion.

Galloway House.
This twelve-room brick mansion in Weiser is listed in the National Register of Historic Places. (*Idaho State Historical Society*)

Knights of Pythias. The unique castle was designed by a Boise architectural firm, Tourtellotte and Company, and built at a total cost of $9,000, from rock quarried along the nearby Weiser River.

From the castle, I zig-zagged around town, stopping at 206 West Main Street to view the beautiful Queen Anne-style house built in 1898 by sheep rancher James Gerwick. I discovered another Queen Anne-style mansion, built in 1900 by Lewis Hall and later bought by Colonel E. M. Heighbo, who was president of the Pacific and Idaho Northern railroad from 1910 to 1919. And at 1120 East Second Street and Hanthorne Avenue, I found the Thomas Galloway house, the former resi-

Oregon Short Line.
The old Oregon Short Line Depot, built in 1895, is one of Weiser's historic landmarks. (*Idaho State Historical Society*)

The Pythian Castle.
The interesting dual-turreted structure, built by thirty Weiser businessmen, was made of rock quarried near the Weiser River. (*Idaho State Historical Society*)

dence of one of the early settlers in the Weiser Valley. The well-preserved twelve-room brick mansion is now listed on the National Register of Historic Places.

Although you can probably spend at least a couple of days wandering Weiser's streets and discovering historically significant structures (check with the Chamber of Commerce for a list of buildings) I was anxious to hit the open road for the country north of Weiser. After an overnight stop at the National Forest Service's Lower Spring Creek Campground north of town, the next morning I headed up U.S. 95.

For about 30 miles I wound through the brown hills of the valley until I topped Midvale Hill, about 2½ miles south of the little town of

Vendome Hotel.
This elegant old hotel stands as a symbol of the bygone days of Weiser. (*Washington County Historical Society*)

The Midvale site represents the southernmost excavated manifestation of the Plateau Indian culture.

Midvale. Here Midvale Hill was the site of extensive excavation in 1963 when relics of early Indian civilizations were discovered. Archaeological studies placed the age of the discoveries from about 3000 B.C. to 1000 B.C.

At the base of the hill the town of Midvale, established in 1870 by lumbermill owner John Reed, sits on the banks of the Weiser River. From Midvale, U.S. 95 parallels the river, continuing north through another small town, Cambridge, marking the turnoff of State Route 71 that cuts west toward Hell's Canyon and a succession of dams: Brownlee, Oxbow, and Hell's Canyon.

Council and Seven Devils Mountains

Instead of taking the turn to the canyon, I continued on the remaining twenty miles into the beautiful Meadows Valley and the town of Council where I had arranged to fly over the canyon with veteran bush pilot Clint Yates of the Council Air Service. By the time I rolled into Council, however, it was late afternoon. The hour and a heavy overcast made it necessary to postpone the flight until the following morning.

Free to explore the town during the remaining hours of the day, I did so and learned that Council, now called the gateway to the magnificent Seven Devils Mountains, takes its name from having at one time been the gathering place for the various Indian tribes—Nez Perce, Umatilla, Shoshone—who inhabited the surrounding area. It was founded in 1876 by George Moser who originally came to the Meadows Valley to farm. Moser was later seriously injured in a grizzly bear attack and, his health shattered, eventually returned to his native Arkansas where he died in 1894.

The next morning, with a heavy overcast still hanging over the area, it looked like I was in for another day of exploration from my motor-home. But just before noon, patches of blue began to appear in the west, and an hour later Clint Yates's little Super Cub with me on board was rolling down the runway.

From Council we set a course northwest toward Hell's Canyon and the Seven Devils Mountains. After about twenty minutes of flying over the snowdusted mountains, we broke over the rim of the canyon at

Hell's Canyon.
An aerial view is the best way to realize the canyon's dramatic scale and the beauty of the Snake River as it rushes through the steep walls of the chasm.

Gateway to Hell's Canyon.
Nestled in the beautiful Meadows Valley, the historic hamlet of Council is the gateway
to Hell's Canyon and the rugged backcountry of the Seven Devils Mountains.

Hell's Canyon Dam and followed the chasm north, high above the
Snake River.

From the air Hell's Canyon is truly an awesome sight. Just above the
dam the walls, although certainly steep, have a slight slope as they
plunge toward the river below. But going north the walls become
steeper and narrower as the canyon nears its deepest point, a 7,900-
foot drop—2,000 feet deeper than the Grand Canyon. Although there
are a number of outfitters who offer excursions into the canyon, and
some of the area is accessible by side roads, an aerial view is really the
best way to fully realize the canyon's dramatic scale. (Aerial excursions
can be arranged at the Council airport.)

Flying under the overcast, we broke into a patch of blue that sent a
shaft of sunlight to reflect off the Snake River far below. It was hard to
believe that the river—a small stream from this altitude—was responsible for carving this magnificent canyon in combination with volcanic
activity, massive uplifts, and millions of years of erosion. This is the
geologic explanation for the formation of the canyon and the Seven
Devils. A much more interesting account is offered in Indian lore.

According to legend, seven powerful giants once inhabited the area, plundering the Indian villages and devouring the children. In an attempt to defend themselves against the giants, the Indians sought the help of Coyote, a god with enormous powers. Coyote, aided by another mighty god, Fox, dug seven deep pits and filled them with a boiling red-yellow liquid. The next time the arrogant giants, with their heads held high, walked near, they failed to see the danger, suddenly slipped into the pits, and sank into the molten liquid. During their struggles to extricate themselves from the pits, the giants spilled the liquid over the surrounding countryside. Finally, Coyote and Fox ended their struggles by changing the giants to mountains. And to make sure no more enemies could attack the Indians living here, Coyote dug a deep trench in front of the mountains, the chasm now known as Hell's Canyon.

Though the view of the snowcapped Seven Devils is also beautiful from the ground, unless you opt for an aerial tour, you'll probably have to settle for watching the sunset over their sharp silhouettes. A road leads west from Council into Seven Devils country, but it is a rough drive that local residents advise only for trucks and four-wheel-drive vehicles.

Some travel may be possible at times for RVers who might want to try the slow drive along the side routes that lead to Bear Junction and Cuprum, established in 1897 at the site of a copper mine, and to Sheep Rock, where you can find some extraordinary views of the canyon. Before attempting any of these routes, however, check locally for road conditions, especially for the status of Kleinschmidt grade. Then, even if you get the go-ahead, proceed slowly; I have found that most people are not familiar enough with the capabilities of RVs to give accurate advice on marginal road conditions.

New Meadows—Home of Packer John

I took to heart the warnings that my motorhome was too large for the trip, and after we touched down in Council I decided to continue on up U.S. 95 to New Meadows. Situated in the heart of Meadow Valley, New Meadows, a town of only a couple hundred population, is rich in history. In June, 1877, the valley became part of the history of the Nez Perce War when a band of marauding Indians attacked a number of the settlers in the area, killing seven men and temporarily driving the surviving family members from the valley.

Ghosts remain, but the one tangible reminder of the valley's early history lies just west of New Meadows on a section of SR 55 that goes to the neighboring town of McCall. Here is Packer John's Cabin State Park and a reproduction of the cabin that played an important role, not only in the history of the area, but also the development of the state.

"Packer" John Walsh carried mail from the Boise Basin to Lewiston, then the most rugged mail route in the entire state. In 1862 he built

"Packer" John's Cabin.
The original of "Packer" John Walsh's cabin is shown in this photo of 1907. Although a reproduction of the original is now in place, it serves as a reminder of its role in Idaho history. (The woman in the photo is Miss Ida M. Hazeltine, primary schoolteacher from New Meadows School, a short distance away.) (*Idaho Historical Society*)

Packer Johns Cabin at Goose Creek, Boise Co.

the little cabin on the banks of Goose Creek to serve as a storage shed for supplies as well as shelter. As the years went by, the cabin became a sort of landmark used by travelers through the area. But in 1863, it achieved more exalted status when it became the site of the first Republican Territorial Convention. It was used for the convention again in 1864, and then in 1865 it became a stopover for a major cattle drive through the valley. Finally, the big gold strike in the Boise Basin in 1865 prompted Packer John to abandon his cabin and try his luck in the Boise gold fields. Local residents maintained the cabin for a long time after that as shelter for travelers and temporary quarters for new settlers in the area. In the early 1900s the cabin began to deteriorate, was restored several times, and was finally taken over by the state.

North to Kimberland Meadows

From the famous cabin I returned to New Meadows and turned north into the valley to follow the road as it parallels the Little Salmon River. About four miles up the highway I turned left across the river into

Kimberland Meadows, a resort development that at first glance appears to be out of place in this pastoral setting. Besides a golf course and a housing development, a campground was also planned as part of the development, but those plans have been shelved indefinitely. However, there is a restaurant here and, because of its excellent fare, it draws patrons from as far away as Boise. At the time of my visit the specialty was continental cuisine, which was indeed superb. Since then I learned that the menu has been changed to feature more traditional American dishes, reportedly every bit as good. So, despite the disappointing news about the campground, the food remains reason enough to stop here.

Zim's Hot Springs

Although no place as yet existed to accommodate RVers at Kimberland Meadows, a stone's throw up the road from the resort I came to the road leading to another valley landmark, Zim's Hot Springs. The springs are a natural geothermal deposit that surface here at about 150°F. In the late 1800s when the site was a homestead, the natural hot springs were used by residents of the valley to scald hogs. Now, cooled to reasonable temperatures by aeration, the waters are captured in a large pool used by residents and RVers to soak aching muscles. Beside the hot springs is a fine campground with full hookups but no cabins. The good news is that it is open year-round allowing you to bask in the warm waters while watching the snow fall on the surrounding mountainsides.

Riggins and Pollock

After a refreshing stop at Zim's, I was ready to continue my trek north to Riggins. From New Meadows, U.S. 95 becomes an officially designated state scenic route, following a generally straight path as it parallels the Little Salmon, climbing out of the Meadows Valley, skirting past

Zim's Hot Springs.
The springs here are a natural geothermal deposit that surface at about 150°F. They were originally used by residents of the valley to scald hogs, but are now used as therapeutic soaking pools.

Soothing Waters.
The waters of Zim's Hot Springs are captured in a large pool that RVers will find soothing to their aching muscles.

the little town of Pollock, and then dropping down through a tree-shaded canyon into Riggins. For those who might want to take a little side trip, a road just north of Pollock leads into the Rapid River Fish Hatchery. Operated by Idaho game and fish personnel, the establishment here is said to be the most successful spring chinook hatchery in the nation. Spawning begins about the second week in August when more than ten million eggs are taken at the hatchery.

About five miles north from the hatchery I crossed the city limits of Riggins. In comparison to New Meadows, Riggins (population 500) seems like a metropolis because of its abundance of tourist accommodations. Once a camping area for Nez Perce Indians, and settled as a trail town in the 1860s, Riggins is now the center for several outfitters who take tourists on pack trips into the backcountry. It is also headquarters for the Salmon River Challenge, a company that organizes some excellent trips on the Salmon and Snake rivers.

In a salute to its lively cowtown past, each year the town also hosts the Riggins Rodeo. Contestants in the rodeo are mostly local ranch hands, but they demonstrate some very professional skills. The whole town and residents of the nearby valleys turn out for the rodeo, which, locals say, "is not so much a rodeo as an excuse to have a party." The festivities are held in May each year, so inquire locally for dates.

Along the Big Salmon

Leaving Riggins behind, I crossed the steel bridge north of town and accompanied the Big Salmon River as it, and the road, cut a path through rocky canyon walls. From here on the drive was exceptionally scenic and correspondingly slow as I kept stopping along the numerous turnouts to take pictures and watch the anglers casting from the gravel banks of the river.

Still following the river, I passed through the hamlet of Lucile, an old mining town named for the daughter of Judge James Ailshie in grati-

Big Salmon.
The Big Salmon River offers breathtaking vistas as it follows its course through rocky canyon walls.

tude for the judge's success in getting a post office for the miners. And about eight miles up the road I paused to read the inscription on the Foskett Memorial. Doctor Wilson A. Foskett was a physician who came to the area in 1897 and served the residents of the nearby town of White Bird and the area ranchers tirelessly for nearly thirty years. He traveled the country first on horseback and later by car, making house calls in all kinds of weather throughout the year. On the night of April 13, 1924, he was called out to deliver a baby in Riggins. Driving home he apparently fell asleep at the wheel of his car and plunged to his death in the Salmon River when his car missed the last curve in the canyon.

White Bird Canyon Monument

Not long after passing this memorial I began the climb up White Bird grade to another memorial with a larger history. Halfway up the grade I pulled the motorhome over at the interpretive center that marks the site of the White Bird Canyon battlefield, one of the crucial conflicts in the famed Nez Perce War.

The foundations for this battle, fought June 17, 1877, and the war were laid in 1860 with the discovery of gold at Pierce, Idaho. As prospectors streamed into the territory, the Nez Perce, led by Chief Joseph, were pressured to revise an 1855 treaty with the U.S. government, which would have drastically reduced their reservation lands from 10,000 to 1,200 square miles. Although some of the chiefs agreed and subsequently signed, Joseph refused and returned to his village. Later the signatures of the other chiefs was deemed null and void by an army lawyer, but efforts to forcibly remove the Nez Perce from the disputed lands continued.

In the meantime, old Chief Joseph died, to be replaced by his son, Joseph. The younger Chief Joseph and the local chief, White Bird, were finally given one month to vacate their lands and move to a new reservation. But before moving out, a number of braves formed a raiding party and, revenging themselves for past grievances, killed at least eighteen settlers at homesteads along the Salmon River.

When the army received word of the raids, they dispatched a force of about 100 men to White Bird Canyon to rout the Indians. Attempting to settle the dispute peaceably, the Nez Perce rode out with a white flag to meet with the soldiers. The soldiers ignored the flag and opened fire. The Indians regrouped and counterattacked. In the ensuing battle the Indians killed more than thirty of the soldiers and captured a large supply of rifles and ammunition. In sharp contrast to the army's losses, none of the Indians were killed.

When news of the battle reached army headquarters, reinforcements were immediately ordered from California, Oregon, Washington, and as far away as Alaska and Georgia. As those soldiers under General Oliver O. Howard moved into Idaho, the Nez Perce War erupted into a full-

For the traveler or history buff, there is a National Park Service folder available detailing a one-hour, fifteen-mile tour that coincides with marker posts that begin at the summit of White Bird Canyon Monument.

"I Will Fight No More Forever."
Chief Joseph of the Nez Perces became the symbol of the heroic fight of his tribe against the overwhelming strength of the U.S. Army. (*Idaho State Historical Society*)

scale conflict. For the next 3½ months the Indians, led by Chief Joseph, who had promised his father he would never surrender, fought their way northward across the Bitterroot Montains toward the Canadian border. In northern Montana, just forty miles from the Canadian border—what the Indians called the "Medicine Line"—Joseph was intercepted by nearly 400 soldiers from Fort Keogh, Montana, under the command of Colonel Nelson A. Miles.

"I Will Fight No More Forever"
Despite being outgunned and surrounded, Joseph fought for five days, inflicting heavy casualties on the soldiers. The army brought in more and more reinforcements, however, along with cannons and the devas-

Photo: Buddy Mays

Mule Deer.
Mule deer are native to many parts of Idaho. The mule deer buck's antlers, which drop and grow back each year, function as both weapon and status symbols. This deer boasts a keen sense of smell and can identify the scent of man, lion, or deer in a whiff.

Chief Joseph, after his surrender, was promised that his people would be sent back to Idaho. Instead they were sent to Indian Territory where many died. General Howard and Colonel Miles protested, and the Nez Perce went to a reservation in Washington Territory.

tating firepower of Hotchkiss guns. Finally, with defeat inevitable, Joseph was forced to surrender, uttering his immortal "I will fight no more forever."

From the vantage point on White Bird Hill I could look down on the valley where it all started. The faded panels that illustrate this first battle provide an excellent pictorial description that brings the White Bird battle to life. Gazing across the rolling hills into the ravines, I could almost hear the sounds of the gunfire and war cries of the Indians.

As I got back in the motorhome and started down the other side of White Bird Hill, I left Idaho's heartland and the ghosts of the Nez Perce behind. But the imagined sounds of the battle and the gallant words of Joseph still echoed in my mind: "I will fight no more forever."

POINTS OF INTEREST: Idaho Tour 4

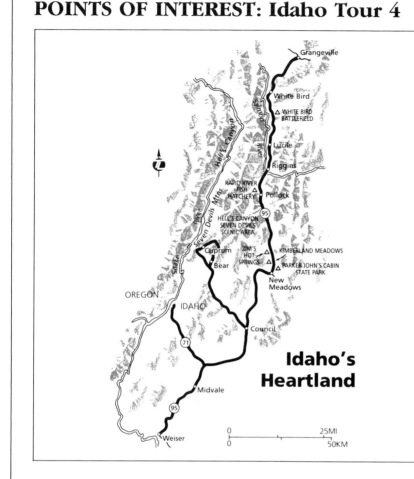

Idaho's Heartland

0   25MI
0   50KM

ACCESS: *I-84, exit 356 or Ontario* exit, north on *U.S. 95.*

INFORMATION: *Idaho's Heartland,* P.O. Box 429, New Meadows, Idaho 83654, (208) 347-2146; *Weiser Chamber of Commerce,* 8 East Idaho Street, Weiser, Idaho 83672, (208) 549-0452; *Riggins City Hall,* Main St., Box 289, Riggins, Idaho 83549, (208) 628-3394.

ANNUAL EVENTS:
Weiser: *National Old Time Fiddlers' Contest,* June; *Weuser Valley Roundup,* June.

Council: *Adams County Little Britches Rodeo,* May; *Porcupine Races,* July 4; *Adams County Fair and Rodeo,* July to August.

Riggins: *Salmon River Rodeo,* May; *Fiddlers Jamboree,* October; *Salmon River Jet Boat Races,* April, June.

MUSEUMS AND GALLERIES:
Weiser: *Fiddlers' Hall of Fame,* 10 East Idaho Street. Open year-round Monday to Friday, 9 A.M. to noon, 1 P.M. to 5 P.M., free. (208) 549-0452.

Council: *Winkler Museum.* Open year-round for free 30-minute guided tour. Inquire locally for hours. (208) 253-4201.

SPECIAL ATTRACTIONS:
Council: *Boise-Cascade Mill,* off U.S. 95 in Council. Open year-round for free 30-minute guided tours. Call for appointment, (208) 253-4225.

OUTFITTERS:
River Adventures, Box 518, Riggins, Idaho 83549, (208) 628-3952.

Salmon River Challenge, Salmon River Route, Riggins, Idaho 83549, (208) 628-3264.

Seven Devils Outfitters, P.O. Box 712, Riggins, Idaho 83549, (208) 628-3478.

Skull Creek Outfitters, Box 604, Council, Idaho 83612, (208) 253-4352.

Wild Horse Trailrides and Stables, P. O. Box 355, New Meadows, Idaho 83654.

RESTAURANTS:
New Meadows: *Kimberland Meadows Restaurant and Lounge,* U.S. 95 at 45th Parallel Drive, (208) 347-2162 (moderate to expensive).

NEARBY ATTRACTIONS:
Hells Canyon National Recreation Area: Reached via routes from I-84 or U.S. 95 (west on SR 71 from Cambridge or gravel road west from Council). The deepest and most rugged canyon in North America, cut by the swift whitewater rapids of the Snake River. For more information write: Hells Canyon, 3620-A Snake River Ave., Lewiston, Idaho, (208) 743-2463. *Nez Perce National Historic Park:* About 60 miles northwest from Grangeville on U. S. 95, this park covers about 7,000 square miles with numerous sites that reflect the Nez Perce history and culture. A visitor center 12 miles east of Lewiston, on U.S. 12 near Spalding, features artifacts of the Nez Perce Nation and the Lewis and Clark Expedition. An audio-visual program on the Nez Perce Indian Nation is presented. Open daily, 8 A.M. to 7 P.M., May 31 to September 1; 8 A.M. to 4:30 P.M. remainder of year; free. (208) 983-1950.

MONTANA

As the fourth largest state in land mass—145,392 square miles—Montana certainly deserves the appellation "the Big Sky Country." But the distinction should also be made that, geographically, Montana is really two states in one. In eastern Montana's great plains country, travelers will indeed find an uninterrupted vista of endless horizon. In western Montana, that horizon is just as likely to be obscured by the Rocky Mountain's majestic snowcapped peaks.

In the eastern part of the state the main attraction for backroad travelers will be a chance to visit firsthand those sites that played such a key role in Montana and United States history. The centerpiece of the eastern tour is the rolling hills of the Custer National Battlefield, where visitors can't help but be moved by the tragic drama played out here more than 100 years ago.

Moving west through the passes of the Rockies, RVers will find the focus shifting from historic events to awesome scenery, none of which is more breathtaking than Montana's natural showpiece, Glacier National Park. French explorer Pierre La Verendrye (also known as de Varennes) called this million-acre wonderland "the land of shining mountains," a phrase that only begins to describe Glacier's magnificence. Sculpted by 10,000 years of glacial activity, Glacier boasts a skyline of jagged peaks, some 200 alpine lakes that shimmer with a deep blue glow, cascading streams, and verdant valleys that blaze with wildflowers.

Of course, there's also history to be explored in Montana's western regions. And, it's possible to recall some of the most colorful events of Montana's past in the backroads and ghost towns around Butte and Helena. In Butte, a city that was known as "the richest hill on earth," you'll be in the heart of Montana's mining country. A visit to the local mining museums will provide a detailed account of Butte's rip-roarin' days as a silver-mining camp, as well as a somewhat—but not much— more sedate role more recently as a copper mining center. A stop in the state capital of Helena provides a glimpse of that city's days as a gold mining camp and the part it played in turning a wild west territory into a state.

In short, Montana is a land of contrasts, where you can hear the wind whistling through a mountain pass or the whisper of battlefield ghosts, view peacefully grazing bison or a Charles Russell sunset, explore a museum or the dusty streets of a crumbling mining camp. The contrasts are endless, and the choices await at each turn on Montana's backroads.

Northwest Montana

"Seashores, plains, deserts, sun-washed and sea-skirted islands, riverscapes—none compare with a mountain . . . a Montana mountain. Its alluvial fans sweep down toward the valley, which it invariably dominates. A mountain . . . is forever so magnificently and perfectly based, all in proportion, its shoulders and snow crown in dimensional harmony with the massive and gently ascending foothills on which it is set."

Chet Huntley, *The Generous Years: Remembrances of a Frontier Boyhood*

Photo: Montana Travel Promotion

Nestled between the Mission and Cabinet mountain ranges, northwest Montana's Flathead Valley lies in the heart of some of that state's most spectacular scenery. Home to the Flathead Indians and the orchards of the famed Flathead cherries, the valley slices northward from Missoula to Glacier National Park and the Canadian border.

Traveling through northwest Montana on I-90 gives few clues to the scenic treasures of the Flathead Valley. Unfortunately, for many travelers heading to Glacier and Canada those treasures remain undiscovered, since most opt for the well-traveled northward routes of U.S. 89 or I-15. That in fact was also my intention until I stopped overnight in Missoula and decided to spend the next morning exploring a few of the city's points of interest before rolling on to Great Falls.

Missoula and the Treasures of Flathead Valley

The next morning at the Missoula Chamber of Commerce office (825 East Front Street), I struck up a conversation with a young woman who, after learning my plans, suggested I try heading back west of town on I-90 to pick up U.S. 93 heading north. She then proceeded to load me down with brochures on Flathead Valley attractions, as well as a good supply of information on Missoula's more interesting sights.

From the chamber office, it was only a short drive over the graceful old iron bridge that spans the Clark Fork River to the University of Montana's tree-lined campus. I wanted to stop here to browse through the campus bookstore in search of additional material on Montana's history and geography. As it turned out, the well-stocked shelves held a wealth of information on the region's Indians, the first white settlements, the state's history, and the geology and geography of the Rockies. For anyone who really wants to get into a serious exploration of Montana the bookstore is a must stop.

Strolling through the campus I was surprised by the predominantly modern architecture of the university buildings. I hadn't expected such a progressive atmosphere for a campus founded in 1895. For that matter, Missoula itself, looking for the most part every bit as modern and progressive as the university campus, was a surprise. I had imagined the city's architecture, attitudes, and institutions to be more rooted in Old West tradition—an assumption that was strengthened after traveling through towns like Butte and Bozeman, which lie within a few hours drive east of Missoula.

Although those towns of the Continental Divide have a strong western flavor stemming from their role in Montana's rip roarin' mining history, Missoula has much different origins. When Montana's gold rush

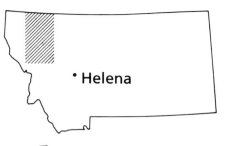

Tour 5 *178 miles*

Side trip to Amish Country, 68 miles

MISSOULA • RAVALLI • NATIONAL BISON RANGE • FLATHEAD LAKE • SOMERS • KALISPELL • LAKE KOOCANUSA • GOING-TO-THE-SUN ROAD • GLACIER NATIONAL PARK

Glaciers.
A view of the glaciers that give the park its name. The glaciers, with sloped, U-shaped valleys and horn-shaped peaks, give a vista of orderly grace. (*Montana Travel Promotion*)

was on, it was the farms of the Flathead and Bitterroot valleys—with Missoula Mills as the commercial center—that fed the miners. As the fortunes of the towns just to the east soared and waned, Missoula, its economy solidly rooted in the more stable soil of commerce, grew in a much less volatile climate.

The city, though, is not without its own colorful past. As with all towns of the western frontier, law and order was a sometime thing in early Missoula. Consequently, the good citizens of the town occasionally took matters into their own hands, and vigilante justice was common. It is the vigilantes who are officially credited with finally bringing law and order to Missoula in 1863 when they captured and hung four notorious "road agents" who had been preying on travelers.

Even when more conventional forms of justice became available, the quality of the court system left something to be desired. According to one story, a man named David O'Keefe was arrested for beating and killing a horse. When he was brought into court, O'Keefe demanded to see the judge's credentials, whereupon the judge produced a deck of playing cards and spread them out on his bench. O'Keefe then asked the judge if he would like to see his credentials. When the judge said yes, O'Keefe unleashed a right hook that sent the judge sprawling. O'Keefe was finally fined $90 for beating the horse and reportedly received hearty congratulations from his friends for giving the judge what he deserved.

The Fort Missoula Complex—"Fort Fizzle"

Of course, all that is in Missoula's past. Today the city, Montana's fourth largest, remains true to its origins as a flourishing hub of commerce. But vestiges of the early days remain. One of the most interesting is the Fort Missoula complex, located on the southwest edge of town at the intersection of South and Reserve Streets.

Built in 1877 at the request of settlers who feared possible conflicts with the neighboring Flathead Indians, the fort was originally intended to be a major outpost for the northwestern United States. Construction had just begun when the company commander, Captain Charles Rawn, received orders to intercept the Nez Perce Indians, who, led by the valiant Chief Joseph, were engaged in a fighting retreat to the Canadian border. Rawn and his men hastily advanced to nearby Lolo Canyon and established makeshift fortifications—later dubbed "Fort Fizzle"—and awaited Joseph and his warriors.

The expected battle never took place, however, because Joseph simply bypassed the army by leading his braves into the Bitterroot Valley. Though Rawn and his men later saw some action in the Nez Perce war, for the time being they returned to Missoula to complete the fort and begin active patrols of the region. In succeeding years the fort was to become home of the experimental bicycle corps of the Twenty-Fifth Infantry, a training center for troops in World War I, and an internment camp for Italian and Japanese prisoners during World War II.

Just 20 miles further down the road from Fort Missoula Military Reservation is the site of St. Mary's Mission/Fort Owen. Established in 1841 at the request of local Flathead Indians who wanted to learn the whites' ways to wealth, it became a very successful farming project. But the priests left in 1850 and sold the mission to Major John Owen who started a trading post. A small part of the fort has been restored.

Fort Missoula.
Most of the land at Fort Missoula is now given over to nonmilitary uses, including the site of the Fort Missoula Historical Museum.

Now, although the fort is home to a small National Guard unit, most of the land is used for nonmilitary purposes, including the Fort Missoula Historical Museum, established in 1975 to preserve the history of the area. The museum is actually a 32-acre site that includes a main exhibit building as well as some restored structures that were part of the original fort. Here the visitor can find detailed information on the Nez Perce war as it swept through northwest Montana, as well as a number of changing exhibits that depict various aspects of local and regional history. Admission is free but donations are welcomed.

Other Missoula Attractions

Besides the old fort, Missoula's other major historical attractions include The Mansion Restaurant, located in the old Greenough Mansion (102 Ben Hogan Drive) and St. Francis Xavier Church (420 West Pine

Street). The mansion, built in 1897 by mining tycoon Thomas Greenough, is constructed largely of wood from native tamaracks. It is now part of the Leisure Highlands Golf Course complex and can be enjoyed by patrons of the restaurant. The church was built in 1889, the same year Montana became a state, and is noted for its graceful steeple and beautiful paintings and stained glass windows.

Perhaps Missoula's biggest attraction is the U.S. Forest Service's Smokejumpers Base, located west of town adjacent to the Johnson-Bell Airport. The largest training center in the nation for Forest Service smokejumpers, the base offers hourly tours during the summer that include movies of the highly disciplined firefighters parachuting onto densely forested slopes to establish a line of defense against the rapidly moving fire. In addition to the film of the smokejumpers in action, there are also exhibits of equipment and still photo displays that demonstrate techniques used in detection and suppression of forest fires.

Everyone agrees a tour of the base is fascinating, but, unfortunately, I wasn't able to make the 24-hour-in-advance appointment required for the tour after Labor Day, so I had to pass it up. Instead, as I headed west of town, I continued past the airport and turned north on U.S. 93.

From the junction with I-90, U.S. 93 cuts north through a rather unremarkable landscape until it begins a short climb up a tree-lined ridge and then, about 12 miles from the interstate, breaks out into the Flathead Valley and the Flathead Indian Reservation. As the route continues up the valley and gradually sweeps west toward Ravalli, a wide open view of the snowcapped Mission Mountains opens out to the east.

The National Bison Range

At Ravalli I paused long enough for lunch at a local cafe and to check my map to mark the turnoff to Moiese and the National Bison Range. Although the map indicated the range was just a few miles off the highway, via SR 200 and 212, getting there proved to be slow going. SR 200 is a rough and narrow road. Buckled by summer heat and pockmarked by winter ice, the road forces RVers to slow down or risk having the contents of their rig spilling into the aisles. SR 212, which must be traversed for the remaining couple of miles to the park entrance, is no better.

But it's worth putting up with the bumps and rattles to get a close look at the magnificent bison herd that roams the open fields here. Actually, about five hundred of the great shaggy beasts, broken into several small herds, graze the slopes of the 19,000-acre range which was established in 1908 in order to save the bison from extinction. Those efforts have been so successful that not only are bison at home on the range but other species thrive here as well, including a substantial elk herd. The area is also an officially designated bird refuge, and ring-necked pheasants, gray partridges, ruffed grouse, and numerous species of wild ducks can be found within its boundaries.

Buffalo Range.
A local resident of the National Bison Range grazes on the 19,000-acre area set aside to
save his species from extinction.

The best way to see the refuge is via the Red Sleep Mountain driving
tour (trailers not permitted) that has been mapped out by park rangers
over nineteen miles of gravel road. The route cuts back and forth up
the side of the gently sloping mountain through the unfenced habitat
of the bison. Along the way are interpretive signs that correspond to
sections in the printed tour brochure.

RVers driving through the range during the summer months should
set aside at least two hours to complete the tour. In the fall, winter,
and early spring the Red Sleep Mountain route is closed, except for
about four miles of road which allow a short driving tour. Following
that route, I was able to view a few cows with young calves in the
corral area and then drive into the midst of a large herd of about thirty
bison that were grazing along Mission Creek.

Because the bison can be unpredictable, the park rangers suggest
that visitors remain in their vehicles even when stopped. But you can
park and get out if you follow the rule of remaining close to your rig. I
couldn't resist the opportunity to get a closer look and stepped out of

Where the Bison Roam.
The American bison is the largest North American land mammal. A mature bull can weigh up to 3,000 pounds, stand over six feet tall, and measure over eleven feet from nose to tail!

the motorhome with my camera. Except for one large bull, the bison, obviously used to travelers and their vehicles, took little notice of me. Every now and then, however, the bull would raise his head, snort and paw the ground, and look menacingly at my rig. After snapping a few pictures I retreated to the motorhome to allow him to return to his peaceful watch over the herd.

Back at the park entrance I turned onto SR 212, driving northwest through the village of Charlo and once again picking up U.S. 93. Heading straight north I rolled through Ronan and on to Polson, at the south end of Flathead Lake.

Flathead Lake—An Indian Legend

This huge lake, 35 miles long and 15 miles wide, with a total of 185 miles of shoreline, is the largest natural freshwater lake west of the Mississippi. According to Indian legend the enormous body of water and its Flathead River outlet are the work of a giant beaver that once lived here in a smaller lake before the Indians arrived. As the beaver grew and grew, so did his need for water. Eventually, his dams caused water to back up and begin to spill out over the south shore. The beaver swam to that end and built a higher dam which spanned the valley from the mountains on the east to those on the west. With this area the lake grew even larger until one night a warm chinook wind melted a deep mountain snowpack and spilled water into the lake in such a huge torrent that it broke the dam and began flowing out to form the Flathead River.

Of course, scientists today postulate the more rational explanation that the lake was formed by glacial action during the last Ice Age. Whatever its origins, the lake is now a recreation and angler's paradise, offering excellent fishing in the summer for Kokanee salmon and lake trout, and Dolly Varden, cutthroat, and salmon in the fall. The lake holds the state record for the largest lake trout—41½ inches in length—caught in Montana. A number of sport fishing outfitters operate on the lake and small boats are available for rental on a daily basis. If you want to just tour the lake on a sightseeing excursion, a 65-foot diesel-powered tour boat, the *Retta Mary,* departs twice daily during the summer from its dock at Polson. A total of nine state-run campgrounds line the shore, and additional camping is available at several private facilities around the lake.

Besides fishing, Flathead Lake is also a major scenic attraction. Driving around the lake on U.S. 93, or on SR 35 along the eastern shore, is slow going because of all the tempting stops to simply admire the lake spread out against the backdrop of the Mission Mountains. In midsummer it can also be slow going because of the numerous cherry stands lining the two lakeshore routes.

The Flathead cherry industry is a result of the microclimate created by the lake. Because of the cooling and warming effects of such a large body of water, the adjacent land area—especially the eastern shore—is an ideal growing region for the cherries. Hundreds of orchards are found here, but most are small and total only about 600 acres in all. Locally, however, this is a major industry and in mid-July, the height of the picking season, the valley attracts scores of visitors who come just for the fresh cherries. For some added fun, visitors can pick their own fruit in a few of the orchards. Watch for the "U-Pick" signs as you drive.

By late September the cherry stands had long been boarded up, but plenty of attractions remained as I made my way northward along the lake's western shore. Passing through several more small towns I left the lake behind at Somers and drove on for about another seven miles to Kalispell.

A Visit to Kalispell

I found Kalispell (population 10,600) to be a town worth exploring. First I made arrangements for a campsite at Glacier Pines Campground (1 mile east of town on SR 35), then drove back to town to pick up information on points of interest. Searching for the Chamber of Commerce office I was immediately struck by the international atmosphere—Canadian and American flags flying side by side.

Just fifty miles south of the border, Kalispell is the largest community in the upper Flathead Valley, and, thanks largely to its inviting woodland setting, is home to a number of artists and craftspeople. It was founded in 1891 by Charles E. Conrad, a wealthy Montanan who had made his fortune in the freight business. Today the Conrad Mansion, located on Woodland Avenue between Third and Fourth streets, remains Kalispell's number one tourist attraction. The twenty-three-room restored Victorian home is said to be one of the best examples of turn-of-the-century luxury in the entire Northwest. After viewing the magnificent furnishings—marble lavatories, Chippendale dining room set, huge canopied four-poster beds—I can see it is a claim that would be hard to dispute. (Closed in winter.)

Kalispell was promoted as an art center during the seventies by noted western artist Ace Powell, who encouraged a number of his artist friends to relocate here. Largely as a result of Powell's efforts, more than fifty professional artists moved to the area. Their works—emphasizing western art—were displayed at a number of galleries around town, as well as during the annual Kalispell Art Show and Auction held each fall. Although most of the artists have gone and the art show is no longer held, a few galleries remain.

After browsing through a few of these galleries, I left town the next morning, heading north once again. At this point, I found that I faced a real dilemma. The fact is there are so many things to see in this part of the Flathead Valley that a traveler literally doesn't know which way to turn. Since my original plans called for taking the SR 40/U.S. 2 turnoff that cuts east to Glacier National Park, I opted for that route.

Sidetrip to an Amish Settlement

For those who might want to consider other options, there are plenty of recreation opportunities around the towns of Whitefish and Columbia Falls. An interesting side trip (which I took later) is on U.S. 93, up through Whitefish to Eureka, Rexford, and Lake Koocanusa. Although this area is noted for some pretty spectacular scenery, a well-kept secret is the fact that the region west of the lake, opposite Rexford, is home to a small Amish settlement.

The settlement is only about twelve years old, established by about twenty families that migrated here from Michigan, Ohio, and Indiana. Only about three or four of those families actually farm the region around the Kootenai River; the rest support the colony by working in cottage industries that include buggy shops, harness shops, and sawmills. A gathering point for members of the colony appears to be the quaint, wood-framed Kootenai General Store that lies along the paved road on the west shore of upper Lake Koocanusa.

An Amish Kitchen.
The immaculate, spare interior of this Amish home features a large kitchen.

Montana's Amish.
The region west of Lake Koocanusa, opposite Rexford, is home to a small Amish settlement. These Amish operate buggy shops, harness shops, and sawmills, maintaining their long-established traditions of life-style and dress.

Glacier National Park—"This Precious Preserve"

Continuing along U.S. 2, with heavy clouds rolling in from the northwest, I paused in Hungry Horse just long enough to refuel and eat a quick lunch before driving to the entrance of Glacier National Park. With snow already on the ground and knowing how fast Montana's weather can change in early fall, I wanted to make sure I got into the park as early as possible to have a full afternoon to view the sights along the famed Going-to-the-Sun Road.

The two-lane road, which has been called the most scenic 50-mile drive in all of North America, twists and turns, oftentimes up steep switchbacks, through the center of the park, climbing to a summit of 6,664-foot Logan Pass. Along the way it allows commanding views of some of the park's fifty glaciers and two hundred sparkling alpine lakes. The route is naturally slow going for RVers, but well worth the time. Because of the park's northern latitude, in early spring and late fall it is a good idea to check on road conditions before proceeding too far into the interior. Large motorhomes and trailers may be prohibited from

Glacier Vista.
A lone mountain goat grazes the slopes, oblivious to his beautiful surroundings. (*Buddy Mays*)

Going-to-the Sun Road.
Described as the most scenic 50-mile drive in North America, this road twists and turns through Glacier National Park up to the summit of Logan Pass at 5,556 feet. (*Montana Travel Promotion*)

going to Logan Pass altogether, and some RVers may find themselves rerouted along U.S. 2 as it loops around the southern edge of the park.

Reflecting on Glacier's beauty, John Muir said, "Give a month at least to this precious preserve. The time will not be taken from the sum of your life. Instead of shortening, it will indefinitely lengthen it and make you truly immortal." Of course, most of us are going to have be content with just a day or two in Glacier. But used to the fullest, it can be enough time to savor at least some of Glacier's wonders.

Established in 1910, Glacier—"The Crown of the Continent"—is part of an international park system that includes Canada's Waterton Lakes

Photo: Gary Wunderwald

National Park. Together the two parks sprawl over more than a million acres of the northern Rockies to form the Waterton-Glacier International Peace Park. The region's topography is the result of a long process of erosion and glacial action that began some fifty million years ago. About three million years ago, during the Ice Age of the Pleistocene epoch, four separate ice fields crept across the area, carving ridges and valleys, and scooping out depressions that later filled with water to form alpine lakes. This process continued off and on for thousands of years until the last Ice Age, which ended about 10,000 years ago. Since that time the glaciers have been gradually diminishing, leav-

A sign at all of Montana's major entrance points reads: "You are coming into the heart of the West where you will cut a lot of mighty interesting old time trails."

ing in their wake the sparkling lakes and beautifully sculpted landscape of the park.

To fully enjoy that landscape you might want to park your rig near one of the many trailheads along the road and hike some of the 700 miles of trails that crisscross the park's interior. People say two of the best day hikes are the 5-mile treks to Grinnell Glacier or Iceberg Lake. You can also take an easy 7½-mile walk that traverses the Highline Trail from Logan Pass north to Granite Park Chalet. Information on

Logan Pass.
At 6,664 feet, Logan Pass is off limits to motorhomes at certain times of the year, when the roads may be impassable. (*Montana Travel Promotion*)

these trails and others can be obtained at the visitor centers at the west and east entrances to the park. Since Glacier is also grizzly bear country, if you plan to do any day hiking, take the time to familiarize yourself with the park rules and warnings about bears. (A bear-alert handout is given to each vehicle at the entrance.) Because of the possibility of bear encounters, during the summer, rangers conduct a number of guided, interpretive hikes for those who may feel more comfortable in a group.

"This Precious Preserve."
Glacier National Park, one of America's most spectacular, contains fifty glaciers, two hundred alpine lakes, and magnificent vistas from its many roads. (*Montana Travel Promotion*)

A Gathering of Eagles

A special annual event is the gathering of eagles at McDonald Creek, giving rise to a ranger-led Eagle Watch Trip that is limited to twelve individuals. For those who check in early it is a chance to view the eagles during their migration from Canada. The birds' arrival in the park coincides with the fall run of Kokanee salmon from Flathead Lake to the creek. The eagles soar and dive along the creek canyon, putting on a remarkable show as they feast on the dying salmon. In 1981 a record 639 eagles were counted during just one day.

RVer's Paradise

Besides wildlife, trails, awesome scenery, quaint trailside chalets, and majestic old lodges, Glacier also boasts some beautiful campgrounds that are usually open from late June and until late September. The presence of these campgrounds makes Glacier a true RVers' paradise, and gives RVers opportunities to linger in the park long after other visitors have been forced to return to their lodgings in one of the nearby towns.

The eagle flies nearest the sun, no other bird flies so near. So he brings down the life of the sun, and the power of the sun, in his wings, and men who see him wheeling are filled with the elation of the sun.

D. H. Lawrence

Photo: Gary Wunderald

Eagle Watch.
One has an opportunity to view a gathering of eagles at McDonald Creek each year. (*Montana Travel Promotion*)

Photo: Louise Trenta

Lake McDonald.
At 3,154 feet, Lake McDonald, on the west side of Glacier National Park, is well into the forested zone. Most of the trees that grow here are the same as those on the Pacific Coast ranges. (*Montana Travel Promotion*)

As one of the fortunate, I planned a stop at one of the park's wooded campgrounds before proceeding the next day to Logan Pass. Remembering Muir's words, I wanted to make the most of my time in Glacier. I discovered, however, that when Muir uttered his reflections on Glacier he probably hadn't reckoned on the capriciousness of the park's fall weather, and certainly hadn't taken into account the September closing of the public campgrounds.

As I drove east along the shores of Lake McDonald, tiny flecks of white began to swirl from the darkening skies. By the time I neared Lake McDonald Lodge it was snowing in earnest; a slanting sheet of white blowing across the road. I had just enough time to turn the motorhome around and head back to West Glacier, crossing the park boundary as Park Service personnel were closing the road to further travel. So I never did get to conquer Logan Pass or spend as much time as I had planned in Glacier. Instead—this time anyway—I too was forced to admire the mountains from a distance. Watching a fresh dusting of snow descend on Glacier's landscape, I remembered other words of Muir: "The winter clouds grow, and bloom, and shed their starry crystals on every leaf and rock."

POINTS OF INTEREST: Montana Tour 5

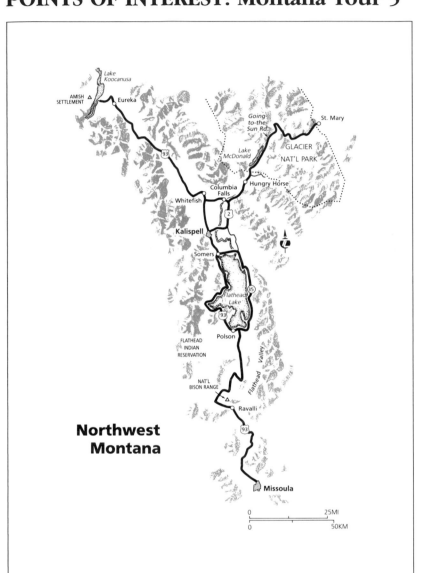

Northwest Montana

0 — 25MI
0 — 50KM

Kalispell: *Glacier International Horse Show,* July; *Northwest Montana Fair,* August.

Whitefish: *Winter Carnival,* February; *Doug Better's Winter Classic,* March; *Stump Town Follies,* May; *Great Lake to Lake Canoe Race,* June; *Whitefish Lake Regatta,* August.

MUSEUMS AND GALLERIES:

Missoula: *Fort Missoula Historical Museum,* at Fort Missoula, south on Reserve Street to South Street West, right to 31st Street. Features central building with historical and Indian artifacts, as well as outdoor exhibits. Open year-round, Tuesday to Sunday, closed holidays except July 4; free (donations asked). (406) 728-3476. *Museum of the Arts,* 335 North Pattee. Tuesday to Sunday, noon to 5 P.M., Friday, 6 P.M. to 8 P.M.; free. (406) 728-0447.

Kalispell: *Conrad Mansion Historic Site Museum,* Woodland Avenue and Third Street. Daily, May 15 to October 15. (406) 755-2166.

ACCESS: *U.S. 10/I-90* at Missoula, north on *U.S. 93.*

INFORMATION: *Missoula Chamber of Commerce,* 825 E. Front St., Missoula, Montana 59801, (406) 543-6623; *Kalispell Chamber of Commerce,* 15 Depot Loop, Kalispell, Montana 59901, (406) 752-6166; *Whitefish Chamber of Commerce,* 525 E. 3rd St., Whitefish, Montana 59937, (406) 862-3501; *Glacier National Park,* West Glacier, Montana 59936, (406) 888-5441.

ANNUAL EVENTS:
Missoula: *Hellgate River Race,* May; *Main Street Spectacular,* May; *Missoula Rose Show,* July; *Rodeo and Horse Races,* August; *Gun Show,* September.

Polson: *Cherry Festival,* May; *Polson Summer Festival,* July.

Photo: Buddy Mays

SPECIAL ATTRACTIONS:

Missoula: *University of Montana,* off University Avenue in eastern part of the city, the 200-acre campus features an excellent bookstore with a number of reference books on local and state history. The bookstore is open year-round, hours vary according to time of year. (406) 243-0211. *St. Francis Xavier Church,* 420 West Pine. Built in 1889, the church is renowned for its outstanding architecture, paintings, and stained glass windows. *Smokejumpers Base Aerial Fire Depot,* seven miles west on West Broadway, then U.S. 93 and SR 200 to site adjacent to Johnson-Bell Airport. Tour includes movie and exhibits on role of smokejumpers in firefighting and prevention. Daily, 9:30 A.M. to 5 P.M., Monday to Friday. 6 tours per day. Reservations; free. (406) 329-4900.

Moiese: *National Bison Range.* More than 18,000 acres which serve as refuge for bison, deer, elk and antelope. Trailers, bicycles, and motorcycles not permitted; motorhome owners should check at information office for road conditions. Open for self-guided tours daily, 8 A.M. to 7 P.M. June 1 to September 30, visitor center open same hours and remains open throughout the year, 8 A.M. to 4:30 P.M., October 1

to June 1. (406) 644-2211. *Glacier National Park.* More than one million acres of what is said to be the finest mountain scenery in North America, the park has some 700 miles of trails and an abundance of wildlife—including grizzly bears. Be sure to check at visitor centers, located at both west and east entrances to the park, for information on bears. Travel season is mid-June to early September, admission to park is $5 per vehicle per week, or annual permit can be purchased for $25. During July and August vehicle combinations longer than 30 feet or wider than 9 feet are prohibited from Going-to-the-Sun Road between Avalanche picnic area and Sun Point parking areas. All other months size limit is 35 feet and 8 feet.

OUTFITTERS:

Curtiss Outfitters, 326 Bench Dr., Kalispell, Montana 59901, (406) 257-6215.

Glacier Raft Company, P.O. Box 264, West Glacier, Montana 59936, (406) 888-5541.

RESTAURANTS:

Missoula: *China Garden Restaurant,* 2100 Stephens, (406) 721-1795 (Chinese-American, moderate).

Kalispell: *The Lighterside Restaurant,* 221 Main Street, (406) 752-3668 (soups and breads a specialty, American and nouvelle cuisine, moderate); *Jason's,* 701 E. Idaho St., (406) 257-7790 (American, moderate); *Terkin's,* 640 E. Idaho St., (406) 755-0322 (homemade pies, moderate); *M.J.'s,* 1600 Hwy 93S. (406) 257-8666 (Senior discounts, moderate).

Whitefish: *Frederic's,* downtown in Remington Hotel, (406) 862-7632 (American, dinner only, prime rib a specialty, moderate); *Stump Town Station,* 115 Central Avenue, (406) 862-4979 (American, family fare, moderate).

NEARBY ATTRACTIONS:

Blackfeet Indian Nation. Located on the east side of Glacier National Park, the Blackfeet Nation occupies 1.5 million acres which includes historic sites such as Camp Disappointment and Ghost Ridge, and features the North American Indian Days celebration held annually during the second week in July. For more information on attractions and special events, contact: Blackfeet Media, P.O. Box 850, Browning, Montana 59417, (406) 338-7179.

THE HEART OF THE MINING COUNTRY
West Central Montana

Hear them knocking—listen—there!
Ghosts of miners—fighting for air.
Faint—far away—down the stope—
Picking the cave in—and no hope.
You hear them knocking in the Elm Orlu,
In Leadville mines, and at Granite, too—
In the Coeur d'Alenes, and the Comstock lodes,
And in soft coal mines, where gas explodes—
Hear them! Listen—quiet—there!
Ghosts of miners—wanting air.

John C. Frohlicher, *Miners (Ghosts)*

Photo: Gary Wunderwald

Butte, Montana, has the unique distinction of being named the ugliest city in America—a "pathetic" community with a "bombed out" look. That may be going a bit too far; and besides, not having been in every ugly city in America I can't say for certain which might qualify for top honors. To be perfectly honest, though, Butte probably is among the finalists. What Butte lacks in looks, however, it makes up for in character. In short, it's a great place to visit, but . . .

Situated in the heart of West Central Montana on the west slope of the Rockies and astride the Continental Divide, Butte (elevation 5,716 feet, population 37,200) began life in 1865 as a placer gold mining camp and quickly earned a reputation as one of the most disreputable settlements in the entire territory. Unlike a number of other gold camps, however, Butte managed to live long enough to outgrow its reputation, thanks to the subsequent discovery of rich deposits of silver and copper.

It was that discovery of copper and the development of the legendary Anaconda Mine that put Butte on the map. From 1882 to 1890 copper production increased from 9 million to 130 million pounds. To meet the mine's growing need for labor, miners poured into Butte, and it is estimated that at one time there may have been as many as 20,000 miners and a total of 100,000 residents in the city.

At the height of the mining activity, Butte was a rough-and-tumble melting pot, with some sixty nationalities represented among the seemingly endless influx of immigrants. By the early 1900s a large boardinghouse district served as home to most of the miners. Also catering to the miners were some five hundred saloons, a number of gambling halls, and a busy red light district where nearly one thousand ladies of the evening operated out of "cribs" in the alleys between Galena and Mercury streets.

In what is sort of a mixed blessing today for Butte, a lot of those old buildings remain. Drive up the hill to "uptown" Butte and the old historic district, look down any street, and you'll be looking past old red brick buildings, many of which are adorned with fading, original hand-painted names and advertisements. The seemingly endless array of old architecture can provide hours of fascinating exploration for those who want to park their rigs and walk Butte's hills and back streets.

The problem is that the preponderance of old, worn buildings gives Butte a generally tawdry appearance—a look that isn't helped at all by the dark overcast skies and cold damp weather that tends to linger in the city. In late September, with temperatures barely topping the 40 degree mark during the day, I remarked to one gas station attendant that it seemed mighty cold for early fall. "Oh, this ain't nothin'," he replied. "Last Christmas it was 51 below, and so far this year we've had snow every month but July."

Ghost Town.
Elkhorn, one of the most well-preserved ghost towns in Montana, has dozens of structures, such as these, still intact. (*Montana Travel Promotion*)

Tour **6** *247 miles*

BUTTE • ELKHORN STATE MONUMENT • HELENA • DEER LODGE • PINTLER SCENIC ROUTE • PHILIPSBURG • GEORGETOWN LAKE • ANACONDA

The Butte Hill that gives the city its name has often been called "the richest hill on earth."

Rail Mining Car.
An old rail mining car in Butte serves as a reminder of the city's past.

Sauerkraut Factory.
Peterson's Sauerkraut Factory reminds visitors of the past life of Butte.

Historic Clutter.
Old wagon wheels, crates, and barrels are just a few of the original artifacts that remain in Butte's unique outdoor World Museum of Mining and Hellroarin' Gulch.

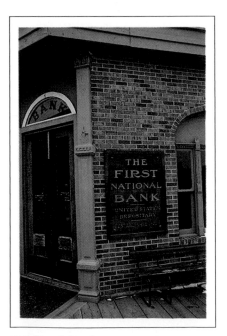

Landmark Bank.
The cornerstone plaque of the First National Bank, Butte, commemorates this historic landmark.

Given all this, why stop in Butte? Well, frankly, some might want to simply pass it by. For me, I get a lot of enjoyment in soaking up the atmosphere of an Old West mining town that still tends to business. What's more, there are some mighty friendly folks here who can make your stay—be it a couple of hours or a couple of days—very pleasant.

Sightseeing Butte and Its Environs

Although Butte remains somewhat of an active mining town, it has set aside some attractions for tourists. The most famous, of course, is the Anaconda Mineral Company's Berkeley Pit, one of the largest copper strip mining operations in the world. Said to be Montana's third most photographed attraction (after Yellowstone's Old Faithful and Glacier National Park's Going-to-the-Sun Road), the pit can be viewed from a platform on Park Street East. Unfortunately, mining operations ceased here in 1981, dealing a major blow to Butte's economy. The pit is now slowly filling with water, and could eventually become one of the deepest lakes in the western United States.

Looking at the Berkeley Pit may inspire you to learn more about Butte's mining past and present. That curiosity can be partly satisfied with a visit to the Mineral Museum located on the campus of Montana Tech, at the opposite end of town on West Park Street. From there you can really get into the spirit of the area's mining history by driving just a little farther west to the World Museum of Mining and Hellroarin' Gulch, also on Park Street, just a quarter mile west of the campus. Here there are some excellent exhibits of a wide variety of mining equipment as well as a very well-done reproduction of an old mining town. Besides the equipment, more than thirty buildings have been erected on the 33-acre site. Plan to spend some time here.

View of the Butte Mining Museum. Several exhibits of mining equipment, as well as a replica of an old mining town, are situated here on a 33-acre site.

Some other sights worth seeing in Butte include the Copper King Mansion at 219 West Granite Street, a beautiful Victorian residence built in the 1880s by Copper King William Clark, and the C. W. Clark Mansion, 108 North Washington, built by William's son in 1898 and now a museum and gallery for local artists. For guided tours of some of Butte's historic sites, you can take a ride on *Old No. 1,* a replica of one of the city's early street cars. Get tickets at the Chamber of Commerce office at 2950 Harrison Avenue.

Berkeley Pit Mine. The massive Berkeley Pit copper mine is dramatic evidence of why Butte was once known as "the richest hill on earth" and the world's greatest mining city. Tires used on some of the equipment dwarf the young visitor. (*Montana Travel Promotion*)

Butte Overview. Still an active mining center, the industry has flourished in Butte since 1862. First a gold-mining camp, then a silver center, the city gained importance with the discovery of copper here. (*Montana Travel Promotion*)

Hellroarin' Gulch.
Trod the wooden sidewalks of Hellroarin' Gulch and let your imagination take you back to the days when miners flocked here to work the Orphan Girl Mine.

On the East Ridge, overlooking Butte, a 90-foot statue of the Virgin Mary has been erected by some citizens of Butte. Our Lady of the Rockies sits atop the Continental Divide, a monument to the idea of one Butte resident, Bob O'Bill. O'Bill conceived of the idea in 1979 as a gift of thanks after his wife recovered from a serious illness. The idea was picked up by others, and the final pieces of the statue were put into place on December 20, 1985.

A few miles east of Butte, I-90 junctions with I-15, which heads north toward Helena (pronounced HEL-an-a), Montana's capital city. The road climbs slightly to Elk Park Pass (6,372 feet) as it crosses the

Elkhorn Edifice.
This crumbling building was once one of the largest structures on Elkhorn's Main Street. (*Montana Travel Promotion*)

Continental Divide, then dips slightly into a grassy valley dotted with the timber of the Deerlodge National Forest.

About 12 miles from the junction of Interstates 90 and 15, the road narrows abruptly from four lanes to two as it continues on into the tiny town of Basin. The area around Basin was at one time some of the richest mining country in the West. A historic marker one mile north of town informs the traveler about information on the gold, silver, copper, lead, and zinc mining that was carried on here from the late 1800s to the middle of this century.

A few miles farther north, the highway once again divides into four lanes as it angles east through Boulder, a town that takes its name from the large rocks strewn about the landscape. When I paused in Boulder for gas, the station attendent recommended a side trip east to Elkhorn State Monument, the site of the former mining town of Elkhorn.

Following the station attendant's advice I drove about 12 miles on SR 69 to a gravel road turnoff that cuts north for about 11 miles to the town located just within the boundaries of the Helena National Forest. It was a good decision. Elkhorn, which is one of the best preserved ghost towns in Montana with dozens of structures still standing, yielded some $32 million in gold and silver during the 1870s. Besides the picturesque, weathered old buildings there is a pioneer cemetery here with well-preserved markers.

Helena—Last Chance Gulch

Back in Boulder I turned north once again on I-15, continuing about 30 miles through the towns of Jefferson City and Clancy into Helena. Along the way I found a couple of other markers worth stopping for.

One, about 16 miles south of the capital, tells about the mule skinners and the colorful language they used to address their teams as they freighted supplies through the area during the gold rush. The sign's narrative notes that the skinners "were plumb fluent when addressing their teams." A second marker, about 10 miles farther up the highway, relates the not-uncommon history of Montana City, a gold rush town that sprang up almost overnight in 1864 and died almost as fast when the gold ran out.

In marked contrast to Butte, Helena has a much more contemporary look. In fact, growth in Helena has been so rapid in recent years that many of the old buildings have been razed to make way for new construction. However, like Billings, Montana's other rapidly growing city, preservationists have managed to rescue a number of old buildings and neighborhoods to assure that Helena's visual history will not vanish from the landscape.

That history began in July, 1864, with a gold strike in what is now the downtown area (specifically, the alley behind the Colwell Building on Last Chance Gulch). By 1870, as mining activity in the area continued, Helena had grown to a population of more than 3,000 and was emerging as one of the major settlements in the territory. As the gold played out near other mining towns, including the then capital of Virginia City, Helena emerged as the territorial seat in 1875, and with the arrival of statehood in 1889, became the state capital.

Exploring the City

As Helena grew in size and importance as a hub city of the Rockies, it also grew in wealth. At one time Helena was said to be the richest city per capita in the country. That early wealth was reflected in the

Helena began life as a boomtown named Last Chance Gulch after gold was discovered in 1864. Many of the early brick and stone structures built in the 1870s and '80s remain, including old stone mansions left behind by some 50 resident millionaires of the time.

Contemporary Helena.
Although preservationists have been successful in saving much of this city's historic past, many historic landmarks have been razed to give way to new construction. (*Montana Travel Promotion*)

growth of some very fashionable neighborhoods around the central business district. An example of the early opulence can be found at the Original Governor's Mansion, at 304 North Ewing. Built in late 1884, the twenty-room mansion was the home of nine governors from 1913 to 1959. It is beautifully decorated with period furnishings and features stained glass windows and ornate wood carvings. A number of other splendid old Victorian homes can be viewed on the west side of town along Madison, Stuart, and Dearborn streets. For those interested in learning more about the early architecture of the city and the history of its various mansions, I would suggest you stop in one of the local bookstores and pick up the two inexpensive volumes of *Helena: Her Historic Homes* by city resident Jean Baucus.

Any visit to Helena has to include a stop at the Capitol Building at 6th and Montana streets. The capitol's cornerstone was laid July 4,

Montana's Capitol Building.
The majestic granite-faced, copper-domed capitol at Helena houses not only the seat of the state's government but also a number of historic works of art. (*Montana Travel Promotion*)

1899, and the copper-domed building, faced with Montana granite, was dedicated July 4, 1902. Inside are a number of historic paintings and statues, including a huge Charles Russell work on the third floor titled *Lewis and Clark Meeting the Flathead Indians at Ross' Hole*. Guided tours of the building are offered daily from Memorial Day through Labor Day.

As a way of getting acquainted with the history of Helena, I found the one-hour trip on *The Last Chancer* tour train was hard to beat. Tours depart every half hour from the Montana State Historical Museum (225 North Roberts), June 1 through Labor Day. One of the more interesting sites along the way is the old fire tower near the Last Chance Gulch pedestrian mall. Called "The Guardian of the Gulch," the tower was one of several used by lookouts to spot fires in the city's business district during its early days. Besides being a historic landmark, the tower now serves as the official city symbol. Also included on the tour is a restored pioneer cabin (218 South Park Street) furnished with authentic pioneer artifacts.

While waiting for the train I took the time to roam through the museum and view exhibits that include an extensive collection of Charles Russell paintings and sculptures. A fascinating display of old photographs taken by frontier photographer F. Jay Haynes made me linger, as did the "Territory Junction" exhibit—a detailed re-creation of a Montana town's main street of the 1880s.

After my get-acquainted train tour, I struck out on foot along Helena's winding main street, Last Chance Gulch, where I could get a closer look at the some of the old downtown buildings. My walking tour also gave me an opportunity to wander through Reeder's Alley, a restored section of the city that now serves as an arts and crafts market for local artists.

After a long day in Helena and an overnight stop at Kim's Marina and Resort (exit 193, off I-15), I turned west out of the city on U.S. 12, gradually climbing out of the scenic Helena Valley to another crossing of the Continental Divide just below MacDonald Pass (6,325 feet). Descending from the pass, through the wooded slopes of the Helena National Forest, I found the road opened up into a four-lane highway for a short distance before narrowing once again just outside the small community of Elliston. West of Elliston I rolled on through valley ranchlands, paralleling, then crossing, the Little Blackfoot River before reaching Garrison and the junction of I-90.

Detour to Deer Lodge and the Pintler Scenic Route

Here travelers have a choice of continuing north to Missoula or south to return to Butte. My plans, which called for a return to Butte to head east over the Rockies, underwent a couple of alterations. I decided to detour north about 21 miles to Drummond to make the return trip along U.S. 10A, a particularly scenic backroad trip designated as the Pintler Scenic Route. But before that, I made another detour 10 miles south on I-90 in order to visit the historic town of Deer Lodge.

At a point on I-90 that is almost exactly midway between Yellowstone and Glacier National Parks, Deer Lodge at first glance appears to be nothing more than the proverbial wide spot in the road. However, this little town of just over 4,000 population—the second oldest in the state—contains three of the most interesting attractions in Montana.

The Towe Ford Museum

Situated side by side on Main Street toward the south end of town are the Towe Ford Museum, which houses the largest collection of Ford Motor Company automobiles in the world, and the historic Old Montana Territorial Prison. At the north end of town, about a two-mile drive from the museum and prison, there is the Grant-Kohrs Ranch, established in the 1860s, and now preserved as a national historic site operated by the National Park Service.

Although I'm not a real car enthusiast I found the Towe Museum was absolutely fascinating and well worth the price of admission. Inside are row upon row of gleaming, perfectly restored and preserved antique automobiles, beginning with a 1903 Model A Runabout, and including some of the latest models to roll off the Ford assembly lines. There are more than 150 vintage cars all collected—and most of them owned—by Edward Towe, a Deer Lodge resident and retired banker, who began the collection in 1952 with the acquisition of a 1923 Model T Roadster.

Towe Ford Museum.
Tin Lizzies occupy just one corner of the Towe Ford Museum in Deer Lodge, where one of the most complete collections of Ford automobiles in the world is housed.

Antique RV.
RVers will be especially interested in Henry Ford's custom camper based on a 1922 Leland Lincoln.

For RVers, the highlight of the tour is the special display that houses Henry Ford's personal camper, a 1922 Leland Lincoln. The camper, given on permanent loan to the museum in 1984, was converted from a limousine to a camper under Ford's personal direction. It was used by the Ford family and the families of Harvey Firestone, John Burroughs, and Thomas Edison on their annual camping trips in the early twenties. Designed primarily to serve as the "chuckwagon" for the campers, this early RV features drawers and cabinets for storage of food and utensils, a freshwater tank, a worktable, four-burner kerosene stove, generator, and refrigerator. Museum director Ernest Hartley told me that when the vehicle arrived at the museum earlier in the year, they were totally amazed to find that many of the utensils, including imported English china, crystal glasses, and sterling silver flatware, were still packed inside just as they had been on the Fords' last outing.

Hartley also said that since the camper only has a total of 2,332 miles on the odometer and was kept in protective storage for the last sixty years, little restoration was required. Besides the camping components, the RV retains all of its original equipment, including tires. The radiator emblem bears the identification "Leland Built," making it one of the rarest vehicles in the Towe collection.

A Trip to the Old Prison

After touring the museum, I returned to the main entrance for a tour of the old prison. Guided tours are offered from June through Labor Day, and the rest of the year visitors are given a booklet that outlines a self-guided tour.

As I started across the compound on this chilly, overcast day, with pockets of snow lying in the shadows of the turreted walls, I couldn't help but feel that the area within the walls was even colder and grayer. That feeling never diminished as I continued through the cell house, the tower, the administration building, and the various other places behind the old stone walls built with convict labor in 1893.

One of the more fascinating stops of the tour is the four-story cell block area which houses one hundred cells, stacked twenty-five to a tier. Preserved here is the cell of "Turkey Pete" who was incarcerated in 1918 for murder and remained in prison until his death in 1967. During that period, Pete's mind slowly deteriorated, and he began to imagine himself a free-wheeling, globe-trotting entrepreneur. That fan-

Old Montana Prison.
Forbidding gray walls surround the Old Montana Prison that held inmates as recently as 1979.

Cell-Block Row.
Rows of cramped, cold cells line the main cell-block building where most of the prisoners were housed in the old prison.

tasy was permitted to flourish when inmates printed checks for him in the prison print shop to finance his "business operations" in a world market that included imaginary dealings with presidents and foreign powers. When he died at the age of eighty-nine, his was the only funeral ever held within the prison walls.

An Example of Old West Ranch Life

The tour of the austere old penitentiary left me ready for a change of pace so I headed back north on Main Street to the Grant-Kohrs Ranch. This 266-acre facility, the remnant of a ranch that once sprawled over thousands of acres across the surrounding valley, contains a number of old buildings that have been restored as living examples of Old West ranch life. Among the fourteen structures, one of the most interesting is the ranch house itself that, when it was built in 1862, was described

Prison Theater.
Within the prison walls the old theater provided inmates with a few hours of diversion in an otherwise dreary existence.

in the *Montana Post* as the finest home in the territory. Many of the original furnishings, acquired over a span of four decades, are still on display. Other highlights include a blacksmith shop, a collection of horse-drawn vehicles, and the ranch hands' bunkhouse. Admission to the ranch is free.

After browsing through the museum, prison, and ranch, I thought I had just about exhausted all the sights in Deer Lodge. However, I found the town also offered an excellent walking tour of the downtown area that features a number of well-preserved historic buildings. A tour brochure is available at the Chamber of Commerce office located at 1171 Main Street.

On the Road to Anaconda

While I would have liked to linger a little longer in Deer Lodge, I decided to push on to reach Drummond so I could start the scenic drive the next morning. After returning to I-90 I drove the thirty miles north to the junction of U.S. 10A and found an overnight stop at the small campground at Drummond City Park.

The next morning, for the first time in several days, the sun broke intermittently through the heavy overcast as I started down the narrow, two-lane highway that winds south through a broad valley of pastureland and fields of alfalfa. About 15 miles south of Drummond I came across a field of large boulders strewn across the landscape on the west side of the road. Scientists believe these huge rocks were deposited by a tremendous flood that swept through the valley after a natural dam that had formed at the end of a glacial lake broke and sent its waters cascading down from the mountains to the east.

A little farther south the road began to run alongside the clear waters of Flint Creek, which flow lazily through the meadows on the west side of the highway. This stream, thanks to a controlled discharge from the Georgetown Lake dam, flows at a fairly high level year round and is said to offer good fishing.

I followed the creek all the way into Philipsburg, a picturesque town of just over 1,000 that was at one time a major supply center for miners. The town is still something of a trade center for area ranchers and, because of its proximity to nearby mountain recreation areas, has become a popular summertime stopover for tourists. Also near Philipsburg are a number of old ghost towns that can be reached via gravel routes. Inquire in town for those that are accessible by RV.

Georgetown Lake Area

Rolling on, I found that just south of town, near the junction of SR 38, the highway turned abruptly east and began a scenic climb through narrow canyon walls to the summit. On top of the grade a couple of roads turn west into the Georgetown Lake recreation area. This lake, which is one of the most popular vacation spots in the whole state, is nestled in a beautiful wooded setting with a number of very pleasant campgrounds lining the shores. Fishing, they say, is excellent.

For me, the lake was a great place to stop for a picnic lunch before proceeding down the grade to Anaconda. Before reaching town, about ten miles west of the city limits, I came upon a historic marker that told the amazing story of how more than $6,500,000 worth of gold was mined within a 500-foot area on the site in 1880. One gold nugget alone, said to be the largest ever found, was valued at the time at more than $10,000.

Anaconda Smelter.
Marcus Daly built the original smelter at the site of the Anaconda mine, which gave its name to the present city.

Anaconda—City of Copper and Restaurants

With such a rich strike so near, it is logical to assume that Anaconda (population 11,500) also grew out of one of Montana's gold rush camps. In fact, the town is a carefully planned community founded in 1883 by copper magnate Marcus Daly, who built a smelter here to process the ore of the Butte region. Originally, the town was named Copperopolis, but the name was later changed, according to this story. The mine in Butte was named Anaconda by Michael Hickey who had served in the Union Army and has once read an editorial by Horace Greeley referring to McClellan's surrounding Lee "like a giant Anaconda." The name fascinated Hickey and he took the name for the claim in Butte. Daly later purchased the Anaconda from Hickey and his brother for $10,000. Anaconda became the new name for the town. Today visitors can see some of the original well-preserved Victorian and Romanesque-style buildings.

Unfortunately, since 1980 when the copper mining activity in the area began to decline, Anaconda's economy has been hard hit. Dismantling of the giant smelter was begun in 1982, and the area on which it stands is being reclaimed. Efforts have been made to save the smelter's giant smokestack—the world's largest at 585 feet—as a monument to Anaconda's mining days. Thus far those efforts have been successful, although some question remains about whether the necessary funds for continued restoration and maintenance can be raised.

Like other towns of the Montana mining country, Anaconda also has a train that takes visitors on a guided tour of the numerous historical sites. Interestingly, though, Anaconda's main claim to fame now is its unlikely emergence as the restaurant capital of western Montana. This small mountain town boasts several supper clubs and a number of other restaurants, cafes, and pastry shops offering remarkably varied bills of fare.

Before leaving Anaconda, I couldn't resist the opportunity to sample some of the town's renowned cuisine. I found a place to park my motorhome and strolled to the Barclay II supper club for a dinner that included the house specialty, a delicious full-cut tenderloin steak served up with a fresh shrimp cocktail, relish tray, pasta, and a steaming baked potato. It was a great way to end a tour of the Pintler Scenic Route and the perfect way to fortify myself for the long drive east over the Rockies to the next horizon in Big Sky Country.

POINTS OF INTEREST: Montana Tour 6

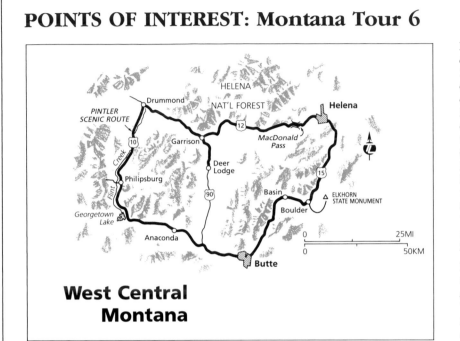

West Central Montana

ACCESS: *I-90 at Butte,* north on *I-15* to Helena, west on *U.S. 12* to Garrison, to *I-90* at Drummond, south on *U.S. 10* Alt., to Anaconda.

INFORMATION: *Anaconda Chamber of Commerce,* 306 E. Park, Anaconda, Montana 59711, (406) 563-2400; *Butte-Silver Box Chamber of Commerce,* 2950 Harrison Avenue, Butte, Montana 59701, (406) 494-5595; *Helena Chamber of Commerce,* 201 East Lyndale, Helena, Montana, (406) 442-4120; *Deer Lodge Chamber of Commerce,* 1171 Main St., Deer Lodge, Montana 59722, (406) 846-2094.

ANNUAL EVENTS:
Butte: *St. Patrick's Day Parade,* March; *Butte Vigilante Rodeo,* July; *Ethnic Festival,* August.

Helena: *Governor's Cup Marathon,* June; *Last Chance Stampede and Fair,* July; *Governor's Cup All-Breed Horse Show,* August; *Western Rendezvous of Art,* August.

Deer Lodge: *Tri-County Fair,* Aug.

Anaconda: *Sno-Fest,* February; *Good Neighbor Days,* December.

MUSEUMS AND GALLERIES:
Butte: *Copper King Mansion,* 219 W. Granite Street. A restored 32-room Victorian mansion that was residence of "Copper King" W. A. Clark. Tours offered daily, year-round, 9 A.M. to 5 P.M. (closed Christmas Day). (406) 782-7580. *Mineral Museum,* on Montana College of Mineral Science and Technology campus. Daily, Memorial Day to Labor Day, 8 A.M. to 5 P.M.; remainder of year, Monday to Friday, 8 A.M. to 5 P.M.; free. (406) 782-8321. *World Museum of Mining and Hell-Roarin' Gulch,* on Park Street, west of college campus. Daily 9 A.M. to 9 P.M., June 15 to Labor Day; Tuesday to Sunday, 10 A.M. to 5 P.M. April 1 to June 14 and after Labor Day to November 1; free. (406) 723-7211. *Arts Chateau,* 321 W. Broadway. Features changing exhibits of regional art; free. Inquire locally for hours.

Helena: *Montana Historical Society Museum,* Library and Archives, 225 North Roberts. Monday to Friday, 8 A.M. to 6 P.M., Saturday, Sunday and Holidays, 9 A.M. to 6 P.M., Memorial Day to Labor Day; remainder of year, Monday to Friday 8 A.M. to 5 P.M., free. (406) 444-2694. *Original Governor's Mansion,* 304 North Ewing. Victorian mansion was home to Montana governors from 1913 to 1959. Guided tours Tuesday to Sunday, noon to 5 P.M., June 1 to August 31; Tuesday to Saturday, noon to 5 P.M. remainder of year; free. (406) 442-3115.

Deer Lodge: *Old Montana Territorial Prison* and *Towe Ford Museum,* 1106 Main Street. Prison: Tours on the hour daily, 8 A.M. to 9 P.M., June 1 to Labor Day; at 8:30 A.M. and 5:30 P.M. remainder of year. (406) 846-3111. *Grant-Kohrs Ranch National Historic Site,* on I-90 business route at north end of town. Features a number of Victorian era buildings, artifacts, and a collection of horse-drawn vehicles. Open daily, year-round from 9 A.M. (closing time varies with season), closed holidays. (406) 846-2070.

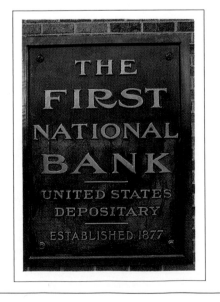

Anaconda: *Copper Village Museum and Art Center,* 8th and Main Streets. Historic exhibits; free. Inquire locally for hours.

SPECIAL ATTRACTIONS:

Butte: *Old No. 1,* departs from Chamber of Commerce office, 2950 Harrison Avenue, four times daily (June 15 to Labor Day) for a 90-minute tour of city.

Butte: *Our Lady of the Rockies,* a 90-foot statue of the Virgin Mary that sits atop the Continental Divide, on the East Ridge overlooking Butte. (A 60-acre park and center is planned for site.) (406) 782-1221.

Helena: *State Capitol,* 6th and Montana Streets. Dedicated in 1902, the copper-domed building houses a number of historic paintings and statues. Open daily, guided tours offered Monday to Saturday 9 A.M. to 5 P.M., Sunday 11 A.M. to 4 P.M. (closed holidays); free. (406) 444-2794. *Last Chancer Tour Train,* leaves 6th and Roberts at the State Historic Museum, daily, 8:30 A.M. to 4:30 P.M. June 1 to Labor Day, on the half hour. Adults $3, children under 12, $2. (406) 442-6880.

OUTFITTERS:

High Country Adventures, P.O. Box 176, Helena, Montana 59624, (406) 443-2842.

Schilla Outfitters of Montana, 807 Cherry Avenue, Helena, Montana 59601, (406) 443-3755.

Montana Fly Goods Company, 330 North Jackson, Helena, Montana 59601, (406) 442-2630.

The Old Pro, 1410 Boston Road, Helena, Montana 59601, (406) 442-3735.

RESTAURANTS:

Butte: *Red Rooster Supper Club,* 3636 Harrison Avenue, (406) 494-4974 (American, moderate); *The Lamplighter,* South Harrison Avenue, west on Highway Department Road, (406) 494-9910 (American, prime rib a specialty, moderate).

Helena: *Tony's Restaurant and Lounge,* 1827 Prospect, (406) 443-0850 (American, inexpensive to moderate); *Skippers,* 1612 Prospect, (406) 449-3474 (seafood specialties, moderate).

Deer Lodge: *Scharf's Family Restaurant,* 819 Main Street (American, moderate).

Anaconda: *The Copper Club,* 500 East Park, (406) 563-9985 (steaks and seafood, moderate to expensive); *Barclay II,* 1300 East Commercial, (406) 563-5541 (American, moderate); *Granny's Kitchen,* 1500 East Commercial (406) 563-2349 (family fare, economical).

Heart of the Big Sky Country

Backward, again and again, they were driven,
Shrinking to close with the lost little band;
Never a cap that had worn the bright Seven
Bowed till its wearer was dead on the strand.
Closer and closer the death circle growing,
Ever the leader's voice, clarion clear,
Rang out his words of encouragement glowing,
"We can but die once, boys,—we'll sell our
lives dear!"

Frederick Whittaker, *Custer's Last Charge*

Whoever dubbed Montana "Big Sky Country" must have been standing somewhere in eastern Montana at the time. Although Montana might be considered one of the Rocky Mountain states, eastern Montana, with its broad expanses of flat farm- and ranchlands, is unmistakably Great Plains country. In just about every direction, you gaze across wide open spaces that sweep toward what seems like an endless horizon.

At times those vistas can become monotonous; take away the road signs and you might think you're driving through Kansas or Nebraska. Still, eastern Montana—specifically the southeast section called Custer Country—is something special. You won't find the scenic beauty of Montana's Rockies here, but you will find a twentieth-century boomtown, Old West history, some of the state's most hospitable natives, and the legendary battlefield where Custer made his famous last stand.

Billings—Hub of Commerce

At a population approaching 70,000, the eastern Montana metropolis of Billings is nearly twice as large as the state's second largest city. Although Billings has a history dating back to the arrival of Frederick Billings and the North Pacific Railroad in 1882, much of its growth is recent. Its present position as the hub of commerce for the northern plains region is due in part to agricultural development, but the real credit goes to the fact that Billings is sitting atop the world's largest coal reserves and amid a number of active oil and gas fields. That fact is clearly evident to anyone approaching Billings on I-90, particularly from the west. Refinery smokestacks belch heavy smoke into the clear blue sky, and bright orange flames from flaring gas light the sky at night.

Greeted by smoke and fire, my first impulse on entering Billings was to find a campsite for an overnight stay and push on the next day toward the wide open spaces east of the city. The next morning, however, I decided to cast first impressions aside and explore the town a little further to see what Billings had to offer beneath its smokestacks.

At the Chamber of Commerce office at 200 North 34th Street I found, as expected, a heavy emphasis on extolling the benefits of Billings's energy-based boom. Unfortunately, in its current efforts to absorb the influx of new residents, some of Billings's heritage has been lost to the wrecker's ball. Recently, though, voices of reason have been heard and a few reminders of the city's past are being preserved amid the modern landscape.

Custer's Fall.
A sunburst breaks through the clouds over the eastern Montana plains to illuminate the weathered stone that marks the spot where Custer fell in the famed Battle of the Little Bighorn.

Photo: Jim Wylder

Modern Billings.
Today a busy hub of commerce, and Montana's largest city, Billings sprang to life in 1882 with the arrival of the North Pacific Railroad.

A program called adaptive reuse was launched a few years ago to help save the few remaining vestiges of Billings's rich past. One beneficiary of this program is the two-story Parmly Billings Memorial Library, located at 2822 Montana Avenue. Constructed between 1899 and 1901 as a memorial to his brother, the building was given to the city by Frederick Billings, city father and president of the Northern Pacific Railroad. The library is now listed in the National Register of Historic Places and currently houses the Western Heritage Center, which features historical exhibits as well as western art.

The old library serves as an introduction to Billings's main historic district, which is centered around what was once the city's original business district. Within the area that stretches from North 26th Street East to North 21st Street, between 1st Avenue north and south of Montana Avenue, are a number of old buildings and antique shops worth exploring. The Carlin Hotel, with its theater pipe organ, is particularly interesting.

If you have a fondness for majestic old homes, as I do, you'll want to stroll through Billings's Westside District, an enclave of some of the city's most magnificent homes. Bounded by Division Street and Fifth

Street West and located between Grand Avenue and Broadwater, the homes here were generally built between 1903 and 1914 by Billings's leading citizens. One of the most outstanding residences is the three-story French Gothic mansion built in 1902 by hotel magnate Preston B. Moss. The entire structure of the reddish-brown brick home, including the glass conservatory, is original. The home remains in the Moss family and is currently occupied by descendants of its builder.

As magnificent as the Moss home is, it is overshadowed by the Castle, undoubtedly the most distinctive residence in all of Billings. Located at 622 North 29th Street, outside the Westside District, the medieval-style building, now a museum, was built in 1903 by real estate developer Austin North. Featuring a round turret, capped by a battlement, a steep pitched roof, and a crow-stepped gable, the Castle is one of the most intriguing historic structures to be found anywhere in the West.

Besides its wealthy and mostly proper aristocrats, Billings also had its share of more colorful early residents. Perhaps the most vivid of all was John "Liver-Eating" Johnson, a trapper and mountain man who was immortalized in the film *Jeremiah Johnson*. According to legend, Johnson earned his peculiar nickname from his penchant for taking bites out of the liver of Crow Indians he killed. As one story goes, Johnson and a few other trappers were ambushed by a Sioux war party along the banks of the Yellowstone River. After a brief battle, the Indians were defeated, whereupon Johnson cut out the liver of one of the dead warriors and ate it. Later Johnson claimed it was all a joke and that he just pretended to take a bite. But, it was too late to shake the nickname, which clung to him even after he became a deputy sheriff.

At the east end of Billings (Montana Avenue to 1st Avenue to U.S. 87/312) more legendary figures of the region's are buried in Boot Hill Cemetery at the base of Chief Black Otter Trail. Here are the graves of twenty-four early residents of Billings who died with their boots on, including "Muggins" Taylor, the scout who carried the first news of Custer's defeat to Fort Ellis.

Billings Castle.
Featuring a round turret, capped by a battlement, the Castle is an intriguing structure that now serves as a museum. (*Billings Area Chamber of Commerce*)

Black Otter Trail

The cemetery lies just off the Black Otter Trail loop drive, a short scenic route that climbs to a point about 500 feet above the valley floor to overlook Billings and the surrounding valley. It's a beautiful drive easily navigated by an RV, although I found it slow going at times for my 35-foot motorhome. Those pulling trailers will want to leave their rigs in a campground or perhaps drop the trailer in the parking lot at Swords Park. Of special interest along the route as it climbs to Kelly Mountain is the grave of Yellowstone Kelly, the legendary Indian scout who also became the subject of a feature film.

After returning from the Black Otter Trail loop, I found another scenic road that travels a short distance east of U. S. 87/312 to the banks of the Yellowstone River and a sandstone bluff known as Sacrifice Cliff.

The story relates that the cliff got its name during the smallpox epidemic of 1837 that swept through the Crow Indian village here. Rather than suffer a slow and agonizing death, a number of Indians jumped from the cliff. Legend also has it that two braves who returned to their village to find it ravaged by the disease decided to offer themselves as a sacrifice to end the epidemic. They blindfolded their horses and rode off the cliff to their deaths. Crow history records that shortly after the sacrifice the epidemic did indeed end.

Hardin and the Custer Battlefield National Monument

From Sacrifice Cliff it is only a short drive back to the highway and then little more than a mile to the junction of the I-90 business route where a turn eastward picks up the interstate (A side trip to Pompey's Pillar can be made by taking I-94 at this junction.) Back on I-90 in less than an hour, I was rolling into Hardin, gateway to the Crow Indian reservation and the most historically significant site in all of eastern Montana—the Custer battlefield.

At slightly more than 3,000 population, Hardin sits right on the border of the Crow Indian reservation and is the seat of government for Big Horn County. The Big Horn County Historical Museum here (off I-90 at Third Street exit and three blocks south) is well worth a stop. Rather than one main museum building, the visitor can enter several exhibits, including a restored 1911 farmhouse, an old German Lutheran church, a barn, a schoolhouse, and an Indian cabin. At just about 15 miles from the entrance to the battlefield, Hardin is the perfect base (Hardin KOA, just north on SR 47) for an unhurried exploration of the area.

Out of Hardin, (exit 510 off of I-90) just about three miles south of the reservation town of Crow Agency, the National Park Service's sign

Custer's Last Stand.
Simple gravestones mark the spot of one of our nation's most impressive battle sites, the Battle of Little Bighorn. At Custer Hill, one can view the valley below, the markers for the men who fell in battle, and, at the top, a large stone monument for the mass grave.

Battlefield Drive.
A winding scenic drive overlooking the Little Bighorn River and the battlefield allows
RVers to follow the course of the historic battle that took place on June 25, 1876.

directed me to the Custer Battlefield National Monument. However,
thanks to road construction and my own preconceived idea of what
the battlefield would look like, I drove right on past the entrance. I
realized my mistake almost immediately, turned the motorhome
around, and headed in the right direction.

Entering the battlefield site along Battlefield Road, I was unprepared
for the wide open, rolling grasslands stretching out for miles in the distance. I had somehow imagined that Custer's men and and Sitting Bull's
braves clashed in a rugged canyon area of rocky outcroppings where
the Indians waited in ambush. It wasn't like that at all.

On June 25, 1876, at about 4 P.M., near the east bank of the Little
Bighorn River, Custer led his Seventh Cavalry command of about 225
men into combat against a force of about 3,000 Sioux Indians under
Chief Sitting Bull. The rest, as they say, is history.

Although the actual battle is remarkable, perhaps even more interesting is the chain of events that brought Custer and his forces to the Little Bighorn in the first place. A fascinating explanation of these events
is contained in an excellent brochure provided free of charge at the
visitor entrance just inside the monument entrance. The Park Service

"A Stone to Mark His Grave."
The stark landscape of the battlefield is
dotted with hundreds of stone markers to
commemorate the spot where each soldier fell.

A Field of Headstones.
Clusters of headstones mark the spot where Custer's Last Stand took place.

recommends that all visitors stop and pick up one of these brochures before proceeding on a tour of the area, and I wholeheartedly agree. The narrative, detailed battle map and beautifully reproduced painting by Eric Von Schmidt bring the events vividly to life.

What isn't fully explained are some of the details of Custer's early career, the events that led up to his command of the Seventh Cavalry, and what may have prompted him to make such a foolhardy grab at glory. Although he was graduated last in his class at West Point, Custer distinguished himself in the field during the Civil War and earned a reputation as a daring commander. He rose to the rank of major general but was reduced to captain after the war ended. Later, because of his friendship with President Andrew Johnson and General Philip Sheridan, Custer was eventually promoted to lieutenant colonel and given a cavalry command at Fort Riley, Kansas. His career began to take off with victories over the Cheyenne and other tribes, but took a dramatic plunge after he testified before Congress on government corruption in the administration of reservation trading posts.

So it may have been with thoughts of recapturing some of his former glory that Custer rode into the valley of the Little Bighorn, accompanied by subordinates Captain Frederick W. Benteen and Major Marcus A. Reno. Exactly what it was that motivated Custer on that day will, of course, never be known. But what is known for sure is that his actions defied all military convention.

Seventh Cavalry Memorial.
A stone pillar atop the highest point in the battlefield honors the members of the Seventh Calvary who lost their lives on this desolate, windswept plain.

The Battle of Little Bighorn

Custer had a total of 600 men in his command, and scouts had reported to him that the Indian forces were greatly superior in numbers. Custer, however, believing his soldiers were equal in fighting strength, pressed on. He then made the fatal decision to divide his forces, reducing his strength even further. He ordered Benteen to take about 120 men on a scouting expedition and had Reno take a similar number of men across the Little Bighorn to begin a diversionary attack on the Indians from the south. Finally, he ordered 129 men to remain in reserve guarding the regiment's supplies. With his depleted forces Custer rode straight into the valley.

Reno-Benteen Marker.
This plaque depicts the failed defense of Captain Frederick Benteen and Major Marcus Reno at the Battle of Little Bighorn.

A Battleground Overview.
From this spot one can view the battle-field to gain a perspective of how the fight was waged.

On the east bank of the river, opposite the main Indian encampment, Custer came under attack. Within a short time his forces were strung out all along the open hills, vulnerable to wave after wave of attack. Chiefs Crazy Horse and Gall led their braves in repeated assaults that claimed the lives of more and more soldiers. In the distance, Reno and Benteen could hear the gunfire and knew that an attack was under way somewhere to the north. But there was no way for them to muster their forces and find Custer to prevent the massacre. With retreat no longer a possibility and reinforcements unable to reach them in time, Custer and his men were forced to stand and fight to the last man.

Custer's Marker.
Although Custer's body was later exhumed and moved to West Point, this stone marks the spot where the general fell.

Pompey's Pillar.
A huge sandstone formation on the Lewis and Clark Trail, Pompey's Pillar National Historic Landmark contains the names and carved inscriptions of the settlers who passed by on their way west. Captain William Clark carved his name here (still visible) in 1806 and named it for the son of his guide, Sakajawea. (*Montana Travel Promotion*)

Driving atop the crest of the hill overlooking the Little Bighorn, on the four-mile route that runs from where Custer fell to where Reno and Benteen held off the Indians until help arrived, it is not hard to imagine the scenes of battle. But what is especially sobering as you pass each weathered headstone that marks the spot where a soldier fell is knowing that it now takes less than 15 minutes to travel the battle-field site in a RV. Yet in 1876, reinforcements were not able to find and aid Custer before he and his troops were wiped out.

Although the site can be traveled easily in a RV, with good parking at the south end at the Reno-Benteen memorial, I found it best to park my rig at the visitor center and then walk back the short distance to

Custer Hill, and the site of the last battle. Here you can look out over the valley below, past the markers noting where Custer and his men fell. A large stone monument on top of the hill which serves as a marker for a mass grave for most of the soldiers who died here. Custer's body was later exhumed and is now buried at West Point. A few veterans of the battle, including Lieutenant John C. Crittenden, are also buried in the neatly kept military cemetery near the visitor center.

The Crow Reservation

After spending nearly a whole day at the monument, I still had time to make a short stop at the nearby reservation town of Crow Agency, where I paused long enough to read the historic highway marker that gives an interesting history of the Crow Indians. During my stop I also learned that unlike a number of other western tribes, the Crows are fairly rich, their land blessed with an abundance of natural resources. From the vast reserves of coal and oil located beneath reservation land, the tribe is paid a royalty which is divided among its members who now number less than 5,000 living within the reservation's boundaries. In August the town comes to life in the annual Crow Fair Celebration and Pow-Wow that brings as many as 5,000 Indians here for festivities that include a re-enactment of the Custer battle.

Bighorn Canyon Recreation Area

From Crow Agency I found a county road heading west to SR 313, where I turned south through the village of Saint Xavier and entered the Bighorn Canyon Recreation Area. This region is a RVer's paradise— a huge, 71-mile-long lake nestled within steep canyon walls behind Yellowtail Dam with plenty of opportunities for fishing, boating, and camping. Yellowtail Dam is the highest dam in the Missouri River basin, and an excellent visitor center contains dioramas depicting construction of the dam as well as historical displays and natural history exhibits. A few miles north of the visitor center you can see the ruins of old Fort C. F. Smith, a military post established in 1866 to protect emigrants on the Bozeman Trail from attack by hostile Cheyenne and Sioux Indians. A marker carries an interesting narrative on an Indian battle dubbed the Hayfield Fight that took place here in 1867.

Chief Plenty Coups State Monument

After a couple of days at the Horseshoe Bend campground (entertaining campfire programs are given on summer weekends by Park Service rangers) I headed west from Saint Xavier on the narrow county road that winds through the Crow Reservation backcountry to the small town of Pryor. Here I paused long enough for a brief tour of Chief Plenty Coups State Monument, a museum honoring the last Crow chief, before turning north to return to Billings.

A gallant warrior who had distinguished himself in years of combat, Chief Planty Coups recounted this tale of his boyhood preparation for battle: "I was playing with some other boys when my grandfather stopped to watch. 'Take off your shirt and leggings,' he said to me. I tore them from my back and legs, and naked, except for my moccasins stood before him. 'Now catch me that yellow butterfly!' he ordered. 'Be quick!' Away I went. How fast these creatures are and how cunning, I thought as I chased the dodging butterfly in and out among the trees and bushes, across streams before I finally caught it. Panting, I returned to my grandfather and offered it to him. 'Now rub its wings over your heart, my son,' he whispered, 'and ask the butterflies to lend you their grace and swiftness.'"

Pictograph Cave

Outside of Billings, seven miles southeast of the city on the small county road that junctions with the route from Pryor, I made one last stop at Pictograph Cave State Monument. The cave from which the site takes its name is filled with strange drawings believed to have been etched in the walls by early Indian inhabitants of the area. The exact meaning and origin of the pictographs remain a mystery.

Back in Billings I returned to the KOA west of town for my final night in the city before heading west to Montana's more scenic Rocky Mountain region. Reflecting on the trip, I recalled that I had almost decided not to go into eastern Montana at all during my wanderings. It was only after meeting a fellow RVer in an Idaho campground a few weeks earlier that I decided it might be worth the drive. He had told me that the area had a lot more to offer than most people were aware of, and, he said, if nothing else, the Custer battlefield was something no one should miss. He was right. Again, words from Frederick Whittaker's poem, *Custer's Last Charge,* echoed in my head:

Comrades, our children shall yet tell their story,
Custer's last charge on the old Sitting Bull;
And ages shall swear that the cup of his glory
Needed but that death to render it full.

Pictograph Cave.
Early Indians are believed to have etched the paintings found on the walls of this historic site. (*Montana Travel Promotion*)

POINTS OF INTEREST: Montana Tour 7

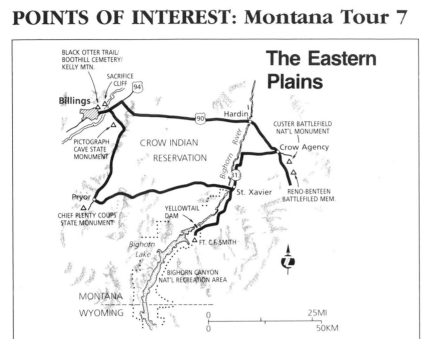

The Eastern Plains

ACCESS: *I-90* at Billings.

INFORMATION: *Billings Chamber of Commerce,* 204 N. Center. Billings, Montana 59103, (406) 245-4111; *Hardin Chamber of Commerce,* Box Q, Hardin, Montana 59034, (406) 665-1672; *Visitor Center,* Rt. 1, Box 12068, Hardin.

ANNUAL EVENTS:

Billings: *Gem and Mineral Show,* April; *Mayfair Auction,* April; *Western Heritage Art Classic,* May; *Spotted Ass Race,* June; *Western Days Parade,* June; *Railroad Days,* July; *Yellowstone Exhibition and Race Meet,* August; *Northern International Stock Show and Rodeo,* October.

Hardin: *Little Big Horn Days,* June; *Country Fun Weekend,* August; *Crow Fair,* August.

MUSEUMS AND GALLERIES:

Billings: *Gallery,* on Emerald Drive in Billings Heights. Displays of contemporary paintings, sculpture, and ceramics. Monday to Saturday, 10 A.M. to 5 P.M., March 1 to December 31, free. *Billings Castle-Austin North Home,* 622 N. 29th Street.

Three-story medieval structure that houses an art gallery. Open year-round, inquire locally for specific hours. *Western Heritage Center,* 2822 Montana Avenue. Exhibits on the history of the American West, and western art. Tuesday to Saturday, 10 A.M. to 5 P.M., Sunday 1 P.M. to 5 P.M., year-round, closed holidays; donations asked. (406) 256-6809. *Yellowstone Museum,* off SR

3 at Logan International Airport. Features Indian and pioneer artifacts, and displays on western life. Tuesday to Saturday 10:30 A.M. to noon, 1 P.M. to 5 P.M., Sunday 2 P.M. to 5 P.M., year-round, closed most holidays; free. (406) 256-6811.

SPECIAL ATTRACTIONS:

Custer Battlefield National Monument, two miles southeast of Crow Agency. Features the historic battle-

field, a national cemetery, and visitor center. Daily, from 8 A.M., year-round (closing time varies according to season), closed January 1, Thanksgiving and Christmas; free. (406) 638-2621. *Big Horn Canyon National Recreation Area,* south from Hardin on SR 313, or take I-90 south of Crow Agency, west on SR 463 to Yellowtail. More than 120,000 acres of recreation area surrounding a scenic 71-mile long lake enclosed in steep canyon walls; boat launching, fishing and camping. Yellowtail Dam visitor center open daily 8 A.M. to 8 P.M., Memorial Day to Labor Day. For further information contact: Superintendent, Bighorn Canyon National Recreation Area, Box 458, Fort Smith, Montana 59035.

RESTAURANTS:

Billings: *Mrs. Butler's Kitchen,* 1005 Grand Ave., (406) 252-4684; homecooking, broasted chicken. *The Granary,* 1500 Poly Drive, (406) 259-3488, located in historic granary.

Hardin: *Bairs Restaurant,* L-90, Crawford Street Exit, Route 1, Hardin, (406) 665-3960.

NEARBY ATTRACTIONS:

Pompeys Pillar National Historic

Photo: Buddy Mays

Lewis and Clark Landmark, 28 miles northeast of Billings off I-94. A huge sandstone formation where Captain William Clark of the Lewis and Clark expedition carved his name in 1806. The pillar also contains hundreds of other names of soldiers and settlers who passed by on their way west. Daily, 8 A.M. to 6 P.M., Memorial Day to Labor Day. *Rosebud Battlefield State Monu-*

ment, east from I-90 at Lodge Grass, on SR 314 near Decker. The site of one of the most important Indian battles in U.S. history—the Battle of Rosebud Creek—this 5,000-acre area was only recently dedicated as a state monument after the land was acquired from local rancher Elmer "Slim" Kobold in 1976. Open daily, year-round, check locally for specific hours..

Index

Page numbers in boldface refer to illustrations in the text.